Bartók for Piano

Bartók for Piano

David Yeomans

Indiana University Press
Bloomington and Indianapolis

Manufactured in the United States of America

Library of Congress Cataloging-in-Publication Data
Yeomans, David, 1938–
Bartók for piano.

Bibliography: p.
Includes index.
1. Bartók, Béla, 1881–1945. Piano music.
2. Piano music—Bibliography. I. Title.
ML134.B18Y4 1988   786.1'092'4   87-45436
ISBN 0-253-31006-7
1 2 3 4 5   92 91 90 89 88

For my mother, Anne
my wife, Sheila
my daughter, Sheryl

CONTENTS

PREFACE

Béla Bartók's contributions to the pianist's repertoire remain unsurpassed in the twentieth century. His published works for solo piano, counting individual selections and movements, total close to four hundred and span a complete spectrum from the most elementary teaching pieces to the most advanced concert repertoire. Although they reflect several centuries of musical style, they contain some of the most original compositional and pianistic idioms of our time.

His legacy for piano is not limited to composition. Bartók was a dedicated and conscientious teacher of piano, having published several influential methods and collections for teaching purposes. In addition, he is responsible for a number of editions of keyboard music, including the *Well-Tempered Clavier* of J. S. Bach, the complete piano sonatas of Mozart, keyboard works of Couperin and of D. Scarlatti, and his own arrangements for piano of organ works by several composers of the Italian Baroque. Bartók has also left an abundance of writings, lectures, and commentaries, much of it having to do with his own ideas on piano playing, teaching, and interpretation, especially of his own piano music. His musical thoughts also emerge from his many recordings, documenting years of his career as a performing pianist.

Bartók also published a vast supply of information that is helpful, often essential, to the proper understanding and rendering of his music. Probably his most important contributions are the multi-volume publications of several thousand folk tunes and texts from his findings in Eastern Europe and the Middle East, which provide melodic origins and helpful clues to the interpretation of his folk-oriented piano music.

A large array of biographies, symposia, dissertations, analytical guides, interpretive guides, and articles about Bartók give additional insights into his creativity and communication. Bartók's piano music, especially his teaching material, is represented in more collections, anthologies, and teaching editions than that of any other twentieth-century composer for the piano.

It is precisely because of the enormity of Bartók's output for piano and the quantity and diversity of material pertaining to it that those engaged in the study and teaching of his piano music are often overwhelmed by the prospect of choosing suitable literature for individual needs and abilities and of gaining access to materials that provide helpful insights into the study and performance of that literature.

Bartók for Piano consolidates this vast network of information pertaining to

Bartók's piano music into a practical and convenient reference. It lists for each work the available editions, timings, difficulty ratings from both a technical and a musical standpoint, translations of the text if the piece derives from folk music, and commentary on Bartók's own performance if the composer has recorded it. Where applicable I have included background information, quotes from Bartók, analyses, suggestions for performance and programming, and suggestions for further study. It is my hope that through this information the Bartók pianist will gain a better understanding of the composer's piano music.

I wish to express my gratitude to the following: Elliott Antokoletz (University of Texas, Austin, TX), Tibor Bachmann (Béla Bartók Society of America), Werner Fuchss (Grandvaux, Switzerland), Maurice Hinson (Southern Baptist Theological Seminary, Louisville, KY), Béla Nagy (Catholic University of America, Washington, DC), György Sándor (Juilliard School of Music, New York, NY), Halsey Stevens (University of Southern California, Los Angeles, CA), and Benjamin Suchoff (Béla Bartók Archives, Lynwood, NY) for their professional advice and encouragement; István Berkes (Budapest, Hungary), Josef Fryščá (Ostrava, Czechoslovakia), Anna Hanusová (Brno, Czechoslovakia), Erika Péter (Budapest), Martha Schäfer (Weimar, East Germany), and Tarina Smoláková (Prague, Czechoslovakia) for their help in translating foreign-language texts; and Washington State University for grant funding in my research for the project.

Bartók for Piano

Introduction

Bartók as Pianist and Piano Teacher

General Observations

No account of Béla Bartók's musical career can ignore his profound and innovative contributions to the literature, performance, and teaching of twentieth-century piano. His compositions for piano reveal a vast repertoire that embraces almost every aspect of musical art, past and present. Bartók had been established as a concert pianist and piano pedagogue for a considerable period of time before his compositions for piano were recognized. Through all avenues of pianistic endeavor, he pushed the frontiers of piano technique and sonority to greater lengths than did any other twentieth-century pianist-composer, an accomplishment carried out with the utmost deliberation and dedication. He was concerned not only with the circumstances confronting the concert pianist but also with the quality of teaching procedures, methods, and materials for the average piano student. This concern is evidenced in his pedagogical works for piano and the fact that his solo piano compositions address themselves equally to all levels of piano study and with more consistency than shown by any major composer in the history of piano writing.

To understand and appreciate fully Bartók's vast legacy, it is necessary to investigate his own disposition as a pianist and teacher as perceived by his family, colleagues, and students.

Bartók's Piano Playing

Most of what has been said or written about Bartók's piano playing is corroborated in the many recordings that have survived from the years 1912 to 1945; perhaps the most common observation, in written accounts or in personal reactions to his recordings, is that his playing always arrived at the inner essence of the music and avoided any shallow virtuosity or frivolous flamboyance. According to György Sándor, Bartók's piano student from 1931:

> There was a universality in the way he interpreted any kind of music, a vital plasticity that somehow made his music breathe, whether it was Bach or Bartók.

As a matter of fact, it seemed that somehow he had found a valid syntax for recreating any musical idiom.[1]

Paul Griffiths amplifies this viewpoint with the following, particularly in regard to Bartók's recordings:

> Bartók can execute prodigious feats of virtuosity, as in his race through Scarlatti's B-flat sonata K. 70, and he can be grandly expressive in things like Liszt's *Sursum corda*. But there is always a feeling that the character emerges from the music rather than the player, and this is something that comes out time and again in first-hand accounts of Bartók at the piano.[2]

Despite the uncontested magnificence of his pianism, most agree that Bartók was not what one would call a colorist with a wide dynamic range or a rich tonal palette. According to Lájos Hernádi, a student of Bartók's from 1924 to 1927, his performances sounded "as if he had carved each piece in stone" but had "an unmatched clearness and plasticity of sound, a sound that was convincing from him alone."[3]

Another notable feature of Bartók's playing, which can be discerned from his recordings, is the virtual absence of any harshness of sound or blatant percussiveness; in fact, many of the loud dynamics or sharply accented syncopations called for in the written score are surprisingly modified in favor of the melodic or linear effect in the Bartók performances. This quality may have resulted from the limited dynamic range of the recording mechanisms of the time or from the mellowness of the pianos Bartók used, but it more likely reflects his refined and sensitive musicianship, far removed from the "hammer-and-tongs" kind of pianism with which Bartók is often associated.

Bartók's Piano Teaching

Almost all of Bartók's pedagogical inclinations were centered around piano. His appointment to the faculty at the Budapest Academy of Music in 1923 was as teacher of piano, not composition, and Bartók steadfastly held to this dictum for the rest of his teaching career. It naturally follows that many of his piano works were consciously designed to speak to the technical and musical problems encountered in the piano studio, with which he himself had considerable experience.

Written accounts of Bartók's teaching style and comments made in interviews with some of his former students, many of them prominent pianists and authors, seem to agree that his main concern was for musical rather than technical solutions. According to Hernádi:

> His teaching was *par excellence* musical: although he never made light of the importance of technical details, fingerings, variants, ways to practise, etc., he thought

the purely musical aspects more important. He believed that at an advanced level the technical details must on the whole be worked out by the students themselves.[4]

Nevertheless, Bartók is described as painstakingly thorough and patient in explaining details of execution; this concern is also evident in the copious interpretive indications found in his own piano music. Ernö Balógh, editor of the G. Schirmer edition of Bartók's piano music, was a student of his from 1909 to 1915 and relates the following:

> Immaculate musicianship was the most important part of his guidance and influence. He clarified the structure of the compositions we played, the intentions of the composer, the basic elements of music and the fundamental knowledge of phrasing.
> He had unlimited patience to explain details of phrasing, rhythm, touch, pedaling. He was unforgiving for the tiniest deviation or sloppiness in rhythm. He was most meticulous about rhythmical proportion, accent and the variety of touch.[5]

Bartók frequently played excerpts for his students during lessons, and he would repeat a phrase an unlimited number of times to explain his musical purpose. His individual manner of playing had a profound influence on his students, some of whom even confessed to inadvertently imitating his playing style in their own performances.[6]

Bartók's piano lessons always started and ended on time; if there was a cancellation, the preceding student would get the benefit of the extra time.[7] Balógh gives a description of a typical lesson:

> Our lesson started with our playing the whole composition without interruption (we had to play everything from memory the very first time we brought it) while he made his corrections on our music with light pencil marks. Then he played the entire composition for us. After this we played again, this time being stopped repeatedly and re-playing each phrase until we performed it to his satisfaction.[8]

Specific Aspects of Bartók's Pianism

Perhaps the most complete account of Bartók's performance instructions is found in Chapter 3 of Benjamin Suchoff's *Guide to Bartók's Mikrokosmos*.[9] The following is a synopsis of symbols and terminology from that and other sources.

Touch

PERCUSSIVE. Implies almost exclusive use of finger motion.
STACCATISSIMO (▾ ▾ ▾). The shortest type of staccato (not to be confused with similar markings of eighteenth- and nineteenth-century keyboard composers, which symbolized merely "staccato").

STACCATO (. . .). Detachment from the shortest in value to half the value of the given note.

NON-LEGATO. Usually implied in the absence of any touch designations; suggests an almost imperceptible separation between the tones.

LEGATO. Indicated by phrase or slur markings and means that tones are to be connected without separation or overlap.

LEGATISSIMO. An exaggerated legato brought about by a slight overlapping of the tones; use of half pedaling suggested.

NON-PERCUSSIVE. Implies hand and arm motion to supplement finger motion.

TENUTO (- - -). A stress marking that attaches melodic importance and increased tonal color to the tone. Tones are played at almost their full value. The key is pressed with a weighted touch rather than struck with the finger.

DOTTED TENUTO (⋮ ⋮ ⋮). A variant of the tenuto marking in which the duration is no less than half the given value, but the note is played with the same weighted touch.

PORTATO (⌒) (erroneously called "portamento"). Similar to the dotted tenuto but played with a suspended rather than a weighted touch.

Dynamics, Accents

SFORZATO (*sf, sff*). The strongest possible accent indication.

MARCATISSIMO (ʌ ʌ ʌ). An accent less strong than sforzato. "A stress of an agogic, emphatic, espressivo character. . . ."[10]

MARCATO (> > >). An accent less strong than marcatissimo.

SYNCOPATIONS. Played with a certain amount of weight and emphasis.

Accents are commensurate with the dynamic that is in effect.

A decrescendo occurs from the first of slurred tones.

A dynamic sign is effective until replaced by another.

In accordance with the speech patterns characteristic of Hungarian and other eastern European languages, the first part of the measure is more likely than not to receive the main emphasis.

Rhythm, Tempo, Metronome

SOSTENUTO. Indicates a sudden ritardando.

FERMATA (⌒). Approximately doubles the value of the note it accompanies.

[Bartók] put great importance on the fact that in a 6/8 rhythm the last eighth should not be too short, and in a dotted 3/4 rhythm . . . the third quarter note should be not too short [and] the upbeat which is the chief indicator of the [main metric pulse] should get its proper share of time, never be rushed.[11]

In 1930, [Bartók] heard a record of a brass band arrangement of his Allegro Barbaro and was appalled not by the transcription but by the speed: it turned out that this . . . piece had been on sale for twelve years with the wrong metronome marking. He thereupon decided to give every movement he wrote . . . a metronome marking. . . .[12]

Phrasing, Musicianship

PHRASE MARKINGS. Curved lines over groups of tones are used to indicate legato and also mark the phrasing. Phrases should be delineated more by dynamic inflection than by separation.

SEPARATING SIGN (|). Occurs between the phrase markings and indicates a slight separation between the phrase indications by way of a staccato at the end of the first phrase.

COMMA ('). Also occurs between the phrase markings and indicates a separation between the phrase indications; here the pause is almost unnoticeable and the time of separation is taken equally from the notes flanking the comma.

RUBATO.

> [Bartók] was against excessive rubatos and ritardandos which prevent the continuous, undisturbed flow of the music. Within this continuous flow some freedom of tempi was permitted, but it had to be in the proper place and in the proper proportion.[13]

Fingering

In all the performance editions the fingerings indicated are Bartók's. In his teaching editions, such as *Mikrokosmos*, his indicated fingerings, no matter how unorthodox, serve pedagogical purposes and should be adhered to. In the more advanced repertoire, the indicated fingerings are usually for a certain musical effect (see *Sonata*, Sz. 80, third movement, mm. 111–118).

> As a whole the fingerings [of the *Well-Tempered Clavier*] bear the stamp of Bartók's own style of playing to so great an extent that the expert can reconstruct the editor's own approach to the instrument from them.[14]

Pedals

Bartók was one of the first composers to introduce the bracket-type pedal indication; it gives a clearer indication of pedal change than does the older "𝄐 . . . ✳" type. It is puzzling why he did not use the brackets more consistently in his later piano works.

> Bartók was for clean use of the pedal without overindulging in its use. On the other hand, he used the soft pedal frequently and encouraged his students to do so. He also used and taught the half pedal for separating changing harmonies or for thinning out a sonority.[15]

Notes

1. *High Fidelity/Musical America*, September 1970, 28.
2. GRIF, p. 114.
3. CROW, p. 156.
4. Ibid.
5. *Etude*, January 1956, 50–51.

6. CROW, p. 156; *Etude*, January 1956, 51; *High Fidelity/Musical America*, September 1970, 28.

7. Ibid., p. 156.

8. *Etude*, January 1956, 51.

9. SUGU, pp. 11–15.

10. CROW, p. 157.

11. *Etude*, January 1956, 51.

12. GRIF, p. 112.

13. *Etude*, January 1956, 51.

14. CROW, p. 158.

15. *Etude*, January 1956, 51.

Using the Survey

The following are explanations of the system of classification and evaluation in the section "Chronological Survey of Bartók's Solo Piano Works":

Title

In view of discrepancies in many of the titles of Bartók's piano works, I have chosen to use the most accurate English-language title of each work at the heading, saving any foreign-language titles for the specific editions in which they are used (see under "Publication").

Opus number. This numbering system, found sporadically in Bartók's published piano works, only goes up to the *Improvisations*, Op. 20, Sz. 74, and in some instances is misleading as to chronology and positive identification (e.g., *Four Dirges*, Sz. 45, has been variously identified as Op. 8, Op. 8b, and Op. 9a). It is partially for this reason that the following numbering system, supplementary to the opus numbers, is used in this text:

Sz. (Szöllösy) number. Since some of Bartók's titles are similar and easily confused (compare *Three Hungarian Folksongs* of 1907 with *Three Hungarian Folk-Tunes* of 1914–1917 and *Two Romanian Dances*, Op. 8a, of 1910 with *Romanian Folk Dances* of 1915), the "Sz. number" is the primary identification system to be used. András Szöllösy (b. 1921) introduced this system in 1957 under the title "Bibliographie des oeuvres musicales et écrits musicologiques de Béla Bartók" (Bibliography of musical works and musicological writings of Béla Bartók) as an appendix to *Bartók: sa vie et son oeuvre* by Bence Szabolcsi. The system is also used in *Béla Bartók* by József Ujfalussy, the *New Grove Dictionary of Music and Musicians*, *Documenta Bartókiana*, recordings of the complete piano works of Bartók by Vox, and a number of other sources. An earlier numbering system issued by Denijs Dille in 1939 is used in the "Chronological List of Works" in Halsey Stevens's *The Life and Music of Béla Bartók*, but new findings in Bartók's early works included in the Szöllösy catalogue have resulted in a numerical discrepancy between it and the Dille catalogue.

Date of composition. It is of special interest that Bartók's piano works be dated and listed in chronological order, since an almost complete biographical perspective of Bartók's musical career can be acquired by this type of survey.

Timing of the entire work. Since performances can vary considerably in tempo, only an approximate timing, mainly for recital planning, is intended here. Exact timings are listed when they are indicated by Bartók in the score.

Range of difficulty. Although each piece and movement is graded in the section entitled "Movements," a composite level is given in the heading to provide a general area of difficulty of the work as a whole, from the lowest number in the collection to the highest. The grading levels are modeled after the system used by Klaus Wolters in *Handbuch der Klavierliteratur zu zwei Händen*:

   1–5:   elementary, easy
   6–10:   intermediate, average difficulty
   11–15:   advanced, difficult

The grading system is approached from two perspectives: the technical (T) and the musical (M). It is important to view both aspects of Bartók's piano music because the technical and musical requirements of a particular piece frequently do not coincide. For instance, some of the simpler folk song settings in works such as *For Children*, Sz. 42, or *Fifteen Hungarian Peasant Songs*, Sz. 71, although technically easy, require substantial musical maturity and sensitivity to convey the *parlando-rubato* type of execution. On the other hand, certain perpetual-motion pieces, such as "Bear Dance" from *Ten Easy Pieces*, Sz. 39, or *Allegro Barbaro*, Sz. 49, are technically difficult but do not ask for a great deal of musical or interpretive sophistication.

Publication

Editions. The editions listed are primarily those still in print or accessible in libraries with a substantial music collection. The firms that first published Bartók's music, Rózsavölgyi and Rózsnyai, have been for the most part taken over by B&H, EMB, and UE and are not listed. The following are the most important publishers of the modern editions of Bartók's piano music, with the abbreviations that identify them:

   Boosey and Hawkes (B&H)
   Editio Musica Budapest (EMB)
   Kalmus-Belwin Mills (K-BM)
   Universal Edition (UE)

Other publishers of Bartók's piano works are Alfred, International, M.C.A., Marks, G. Schirmer, and Schott.

Appearance in teaching editions and collections. Since Bartók is represented in more teaching editions and anthologies for the piano than is any other twentieth-century composer, it is inevitable that these publications vary considerably in quality. Therefore, in addition to the listing of all available published collections in this section, a critical survey of them is given in Appendix D.

Transcriptions for and from other media. Because of the universal appeal of Bartók's piano music, much of it, especially the folk-oriented variety, has been transcribed for other vocal or instrumental media, by Bartók himself as well as by others. The pianist can gain much interpretive insight from these transcriptions.

Additional pertinent commentary and related publications. This section includes published and unpublished supplementary information on the work being surveyed. This material contains, when applicable, Bartók's own commentaries on the publication of the work; peculiarities in certain editions of the work, such as misprints or irresponsible editing; revised editions of the work by Bartók himself; the existence of facsimile reproductions of manuscripts or early editions of the work; the appearance of the work as a whole or in part in other publications; and important written material on the work.

Commentary

The purpose of this section is to provide a sense of biographical, historical, and stylistic perspective; to include pertinent commentary from Bartók and other authoritative sources; to evaluate the composition's overall technical–musical challenges; and to suggest programming possibilities.

Movements

Number, title, tempo marking, timing. Additional designations such as alternate numbering systems or tempo markings from other publications are included in this section. Timings are explained above in the section "Timing of the Entire Work."

Level of difficulty. See above, "Range of difficulty." Individual pieces receive their own ratings because of the wide range of difficulty in some of Bartók's piano cycles. A plus sign after a technical rating (T15+, for example) is a precautionary indication that the piece requires an unusual degree of physical exertion and endurance that may in time cause extreme muscular stress and even injury.

Folk origin. Of the 393 individual movements in Bartók's solo piano music, 189, or roughly 48 percent, make use of authentic peasant folk songs and dances of Eastern Europe; this percentage does not take into account the abundance of additional piano works that include quasi-folk material of no specific origin. It is therefore valuable to the Bartók pianist to have an understanding of national characteristics of the folk music being used; a familiarity with the syllable, phrase, and verse structure of the music; and a knowledge of at least the emotional message of the text, if not a literal translation, to aid in interpretation.

The following is a general survey of folk music characteristics listed by nationality, from the most to the least frequently used in Bartók's piano music:

HUNGARIAN. Not to be confused with Gypsy music, which, although considered by Bartók genuinely Hungarian, was created by "Hungarian music amateurs who belong to the ruling class."[1] Stylistically, Hungarian folk music of the purely peasant variety is divided into three categories:

OLD STYLE. Slow tempo, *parlando-rubato* (declamatory, free) interpretation, lavish vocal embellishment, four lines of from six to twelve equal syllables, lack of an anacrusis or upbeat (this is a distinguishing feature of Hungarian folk music in general), pentatonic scale patterns and dark modes, and a generally intense, mournful text and musical delivery. Mostly sung or played by elderly peasants continuing a musical tradition that has been in existence for thousands of years.
NEW STYLE. Fast tempo, *tempo-giusto* (strict tempo) interpretation, four lines (AAAA, AABA, ABBA) with an expanded number of syllables (up to 22), the last melodic line identical to the first, modes extended to include major and harmonic minor because of Western influences, more spirited text content and musical delivery. Mostly sung or played by younger peasants continuing a tradition that began only around the mid-nineteenth century.
MIXED STYLE. A variety of melodic types with no unity of style, subject to Slovakian and Western European influences, four lines with variable syllabization, frequent major and minor modes, typical rhythm of two eighth notes and a quarter note, ceremonial atmosphere (wedding, harvest, Easter, Christmas), and a generally more spirited and lighter character than Old Style tunes.

A thorough explanation and inventory of Hungarian peasant folk music is found in Bartók's *The Hungarian Folk Song* (BBHU) and Somfai's *Documenta Bartókiana*, Vol. VI (SODO); use of original Hungarian folk material is found in Bartók's published piano works Sz. 35a, 38, 39, 42 (Vol. I), 53, 66, 71, 74, 105, and 107.

ROMANIAN. According to Bartók, most of the Romanian folk material he collected and used as models for his piano compositions had originated from territories previously belonging to Hungary[2] (this explains the eventual deletion of "from Hungary" from the title *Romanian Folk Dances*, Sz. 56). Although grouped into five classifications according to medium or function, only two apply directly to Bartók's Romanian-based piano music:

COLINDE, or Christmas carols. See the commentary on *Romanian Christmas Songs*, Sz. 57, for an explanation of characteristics.
DANCE SONGS. Usually without text; played on instruments such as the peasant

violin or flute. Most of Bartók's Romanian-based piano music is characterized by simple and regular structures, usually of four melody sections, and much repetition and development. Other features include frequent use of the anacrusis (which is missing in Hungarian models); rhythmic combinations of an eighth note and two sixteenths; a compelling rhythmic drive; emphasis on the lighter modes, such as major, Mixolydian, and Lydian; and occasional use of scale patterns that suggest Arabic influence (see Sz. 56, Nos. 3 and 4).

A thorough explanation and inventory of Romanian peasant folk music is found in Bartók's *Rumanian Folk Music*, Vols. I and IV (BBRO), and Somfai's *Documenta Bartókiana*, Vol. VI (SODO). Use of original Romanian folk material is found in Bartók's published piano works Sz. 44, 55, 56, 57, and 105.

SLOVAKIAN. According to Bartók, most of the Slovakian folk material he collected and used as models for his compositions came from a people who live in the eastern half of Czechoslovakia, formerly a region known as North Hungary.[3] The melodies are classified as follows:

THE OLDEST MELODIES, CONSISTING OF SHEPHERD AND CEREMONIAL SONGS. The former have an improvised character, free form, lines of up to six syllables, *parlando-rubato* style, Mixolydian mode, and a one-octave range; the latter, also with six-syllable lines in a *parlando-rubato* style, are in variable modes and have characteristic intervals of the major third followed by the augmented fourth.
MELODIES OF UNEQUAL METER AND FORM. Usually in Lydian mode and *tempo-giusto* style, with three-part phrases. They show a close affinity to Czech and the Mixed Style of Hungarian folk melodies.
MODERN MELODIES. Strongly influenced by the New Style Hungarian folk melodies, especially with regard to their rhythmic characteristics.

A thorough explanation and inventory of Slovakian peasant folk music is found in Bartók's *Slovenské L'udové Piesne* (Slovakian folk songs), Vols. I and II (BBSL), and Somfai's *Documenta Bartókiana*, Vol. VI (SODO). Use of original Slovakian folk material is found in Bartók's published piano works Sz. 38, 42 (Vol. II), and 84.

OTHER NATIONALITIES. One also finds occasional use of both authentic and freely composed Bulgarian (Sz. 107), Yugoslavian (Sz. 107), Ukrainian (Sz. 105), and Arabic (Sz. 62 and 77) folk material in Bartók's piano works. Characteristics of these folk styles are explained in the commentary on the specific examples that make use of them.

For most of the examples based on original folk tunes, short English paraphrases of the text provide the essence of the mood and subject. Reference is made to the sources in which the texts are presented in full, both in English translation and in their original languages. When no text is included, it is either unavailable or unfit to print because of offensive language or subject matter.

Analysis. Each piece is identified as to key center and, in the case of folk-song arrangements, the mode or scale type. The key-center listings exemplify the consistent logic and clarity of Bartók's tonal organization. The following table identifies the mode or scale types found in folk music:

Dorian	D–D, white keys of the piano
	E–E, 2 sharps (in the normal sequence of the D-major key signature)
	F–F, 3 flats (E-flat major)
	G–G, 1 flat (F major)
	A–A, 1 sharp (G major)
	B–B, 3 sharps (A major)
	C–C, 2 flats (B-flat major)
Phrygian	E–E, white keys
	F–F, 5 flats (D-flat major)
	G–G, 3 flats (E-flat major)
	A–A, 1 flat (F major)
	B–B, 1 sharp (G major)
	C–C, 4 flats (A-flat major)
	D–D, 2 flats (B-flat major)
Lydian	F–F, white keys
	G–G, 2 sharps (D major)
	A–A, 4 sharps (E major)
	B–B, 6 sharps (F-sharp major)
	C–C, 1 sharp (G major)
	D–D, 3 sharps (A major)
	E–E, 5 sharps (B major)
Mixolydian	G–G, white keys
	A–A, 2 sharps (D major)
	B–B, 4 sharps (E major)
	C–C, 1 flat (F major)
	D–D, 1 sharp (G major)
	E–E, 3 sharps (A major)
	F–F, 2 flats (B-flat major)
Aeolian (natural minor)	A–A, white keys
	B–B, 2 sharps (D major)
	C–C, 3 flats (E-flat major)
	D–D, 1 flat (F major)
	E–E, 1 sharp (G major)
	F–F, 4 flats (A-flat major)

	G–G, 2 flats (B-flat major)
Ionian (major)	C–C, white keys (all successive starting tones have major key signatures).
Pentatonic	Any scale that contains five tones and lacks semitones (e.g., the black keys of the piano, although numerous other interval combinations are possible).
Non-diatonic	Any seven-tone scale that does not conform to the major–minor or modal interval relationships (any combination of five whole tones and two semitones).

Each piece is surveyed with regard to some or all of the following aspects: texture, structure,[4] unusual stylistic features, specific technical or musical difficulties, performance suggestions, programming possibilities, and applicability to the specific pianist's level or aptitudes. Statements by Bartók himself and appropriate commentary from noted Bartók authorities on the particular example are included in this section.

Recordings

This section lists and analyzes most of the existing recordings that Bartók made of his piano music. Although many other recordings of high merit have been produced over the years, most notably the complete editions of Bartók's piano works by Vox and Hungaroton,[5] the composer's own performances seem to give the most accurate and revealing insights into his piano music.

The listings include the volume, side, and band of each piece in the Hungaroton collection *Centenary Edition of Bartók's Records* (1981), the record label and date of the original LP release produced by Hungaroton, and recordings by Bartók in other collections. Analyses include discussion of distinctive features of each performance that might be of value to the reader.

Notes

(Throughout this volume, works quoted in the text are referred to by their abbreviatiohs. Full citations are given in the Bibliography.)

1. BBES, p. 71.
2. Ibid., p. 115.
3. Ibid, pp. 128–129.
4. Regarding pieces based on original folk music and cast in variation form, the original folk tune is considered the "theme," and the example begins with the first variation. This method has precedents in variation forms where the theme is a preexisting popular melody.
5. For a comparative survey of other recordings of Bartók's piano music, see Jeremy Noble, "Bartók Recordings," *High Fidelity*, March 1981, 45–53.

Chronological Survey

of Bartók's

Solo Piano Works

Funeral March from *Kossuth*

Sz. 21
1903
T11 M10
4'

Publication

Included in:
Balógh, ed. *Bartók. Selected Works for the Piano* (Schrimer).
BBPI, Series I.
Transcribed by Bartók from sections 9 and 10 of the original orchestral setting
of the same name (*Kossuth*, Symphonic Poem for Orchestra, Sz. 21, 1903).

Commentary

The piano arrangement by Bartók of this orchestral excerpt was made at a
time in his career when he was transcribing and performing piano versions of
orchestral works by other composers, most notably those of Richard Strauss (*Ein
Heldenleben, Also Sprach Zarathustra*). The background of the present example is
best expressed in Bartók's own program notes for the first performance of the
orchestral work in 1904:

> The leader [of the Hungarian revolution against the sovereignty of the
> Austrians and the Habsburg dynasty] was Louis Kossuth. As Austria saw, in
> 1849, that the war was going against her, she concluded an alliance with Russia.
> A crushing blow was inflicted upon the Hungarian Army, and the hope of an in-
> dependent Hungarian kingdom was shattered—apparently for ever.[1]

The "Funeral March," sections 9 and 10 of the orchestral version, reflects
the tragedy of defeat: "All is finished. Hungary lies in deepest woe, in deepest
mourning—" and "A hopeless silence reigns."[2]

Movement

Lento—Adagio molto.
Key center A. Introduction followed by subject marked "Adagio molto,"
which undergoes intensive melodic and harmonic variation. Ostinato in double-
dotted rhythms forms the rhythmic basis for the work, often combined with a

rhythmic pattern in triplets. A series of indeterminate (non-metric) arpeggio figurations in the left hand before the coda. Pianist must be able to coordinate these characteristic rhythmic patterns while maintaining a steady metric pulse throughout. A strong stylistic kinship between this piece and Liszt's "Funérailles" from *Harmonies poétiques et religieuses.*

Notes

1. BBES, p. 399.
2. Ibid., p. 403.

Four Piano Pieces

Sz. 22
1903
T10–14 M10–12
26' 50"

Publication

Available separately:
EMB, as *Négy Zongoradarab* (No. 1 also published separately).
K-BM (Nos. 1, 2–3, and 4 also published separately).

Included in:
K-BM, publ., *Bartók. An Album for Piano Solo* (No. 2).
BBPI, Series I.

No. 4 transcribed by Bartók for piano and orchestra (Op. 2, Sz. 28, 1904–1905, EMB). Although the basic structure remains similar to the solo piano version, the arrangement includes an introductory "Adagio ma non troppo," which does not appear in the solo version.

Commentary

This cycle, written at the end of Bartók's studies at the Academy of Music in Budapest, shows a marked affinity to the Romantic traditions of Liszt, Brahms, and Richard Strauss. Although the pieces are not representative of the mainstream of Bartók's mature compositional style, they are worthy of study and performance for insights into some of the nineteenth-century influences in his early compositional career. They are stunningly virtuosic, make use of an abundance of technical figurations, and display a bold and extroverted musical outlook. One or two pieces from the cycle could be studied and performed as alternatives to the more standard and better-known works of the nineteenth century.

Movements

No. 1. Study for the Left Hand (*Tanulmány balkézre*). Allegro. (8' 50") T13 M10

Key center B-flat. Sonata-rondo design, originally conceived as a movement in a large-scale piano sonata. Dedicated to Bartók's piano teacher at the Academy, István Thoman, but written under the stimulus of one Géza Zichy, a concert pianist who lost his right arm in a hunting accident but subsequently continued his concert career as a left-hand pianist. Sweeping arpeggio figurations and octave passages which run the gamut of the keyboard. Although relatively unknown, this piece could be a welcome addition to the select core of piano works for the left hand, notably those of Ravel, Prokofieff, and Scriabin.

No. 2. Fantasy I (*I. Ábránd*). Andante, quasi Adagio. (4' 50") T11 M10

Key center C. Dedicated to Emma Gruber, who married Zoltán Kodály in 1910 and who "at that time was one of the most inspiring personalities linking the traditional and modern periods in the musical life of Hungary."[1] Free structure, elegiac mood, influence of Richard Strauss and Brahms. Much sweeping arpeggiation in the left hand, parallel chords and octaves, counterrhythms. The second beat of m. 4 should obviously read B-natural.

No. 3. Fantasy II (*II. Ábránd*). Andante. (4' 10") T10 M10

Key center A. Loosely constructed ABA form; extensive melodic variation of the opening motive throughout the piece, much like that found in the intermezzi of Brahms. Parallel intervals, mostly in thirds and octaves, abound. The indication "Ped. (prolongation) . . . sempre . . ." at m. 27 should be observed literally until the change of harmony at m. 31. The most compact and ingeniously constructed of the set, and probably the most worthy of serious study.

No. 4. Scherzo. Allegro vivace. (9') T14 M12

Key center E. Dedicated to Ernö Dohnányi, a major influence on Bartók's early career and a well-known composer in his own right. Sonata-rondo form, one of Bartók's longest single-movement solo piano pieces, a precursor of the more mature and elaborate *Rhapsody*, Op. 1, Sz. 26, composed one year later. Note the metric discrepancies between the staves and non-coincident bar lines in the "Vivace molto" (beginning in m. 244) and the "Molto vivace" (beginning in m. 431); maintain the preceding meter as the primary metric unit in these passages (2/4 in the former, 3/8 in the latter). Scale passages, parallel thirds, parallel and interlocking octaves; a bravura, full-textured virtuoso piece reminiscent of the scherzo movements of early Brahms. Anyone who attempts this piece should be familiar with the version for piano and orchestra.

Note

1. Hungaroton SLPX 1300, Vol. I, p. 6.

Rhapsody

Op. 1, Sz. 26
1904
T15 M13
20' 45"

Publication

Available separately:
EMB
UE
Included in:
BBPI, Series I.

Transcribed by Bartók for piano and orchestra (Op. 1, Sz. 27, 1904, EMB). Although the basic structure remains similar to the solo piano version, the arrangement includes an introductory "Adagio molto-Doppio movimento" of 41 measures.

Commentary

The most significant of Bartók's post-Romantic piano works, the *Rhapsody* is the only piece from that period that the composer continued to include in his solo piano recitals. He entered the piano and orchestra setting in the competition for the Rubinstein Prize in 1905—further testimony to its importance among his early works. It is referred to as "a bravura piece par excellence, . . .

the last echoes of the Franz Liszt–Anton Rubinstein technique."[1] With the exception of the *Elegies*, Op. 8b, Sz. 41, the *Rhapsody* represents Bartók's last composition under the direct influence of the Romantic tradition. By this time Bartók had already turned his attention to peasant folk music, French Impressionism, and more concise and progressive compositional techniques, all of which served as strong musical stimuli during the rest of his creative life.

Movement

Mesto.

Key center D. Freely composed in two large sections, the first corresponding to the *lassú* (slow introductory fantasy), the second to the *friss* (fast energetic dance); both are the main components of the *verbunkos*, a recruiting dance of the Hungarian soldiers. The *lassú* ("Mesto") has a distinctly Lisztian flavor; it is held together by extensive melodic development of the opening theme in a highly improvisatory and ornamented manner. The following *friss* section (beginning in m. 118) starts "Tranquillo" and progresses through several tempo changes to the "Presto" (beginning in m. 431). It maintains a lively duple-meter dance character until the triumphant return (in m. 564) of the *lassú* theme, this time in D major, and finally subsides to the quiet and contemplative character of the opening. For the pianist of the highest virtuoso attainments; need for advanced technical equipment, the ability to hold together a large and heterogeneous structure, and a keen stylistic grasp of a variety of Gypsy musical temperaments. Enormous demands on octave, chord, arpeggio, and double-note technique; many awkward passages conceived orchestrally. In either setting, the work as a whole surpasses many of Liszt's Hungarian rhapsodies in difficulty and scope.

Note

1. FENY, p. 32.

Three Hungarian Folksongs
from Csík

Sz. 35a
1907
T4-6 M5-9
3' 10"

Publication

Available separately:
EMB, as Három Csíkmegyei Népdal
K-BM

Included in:
EMB, publ., *Bartók Béla. Album*, Vol. II.
K-BM, publ., *Bartók. An Album for Piano Solo*.
BBPI, Series I.

Transcribed by János Szebenyi for flute and piano (1955); by György Balassa
for clarinet and piano (1955); by T. Szeszler for oboe and piano; and by Denes
Dille for recorder and piano.

Commentary

These three miniatures represent the first adaptations by Bartók of Hungarian
peasant folk music to the medium of solo piano. He describes their derivation
as "unaltered (transcribed from phonograph record) peasant flute music,
provided with accompaniment. . . ."[1] The melodies are highly ornamented and
the accompaniments simple and chordal. The set can be effectively programmed
as a companion to one of Bartók's folk-dance cycles or as a recital opener.

Movements

The folk texts are excerpted and paraphrased from the English translations
in BBHU and BBPI (Series I); complete texts in the original language appear
in BBHU, BBPI (Series I), and SODO.

No. 1. Rubato. (1' 25") T4 M9
Key center B; Dorian mode. A highly ornamented and rhythmically free

melody over arpeggiated accompaniment. Notated trills and sliding figurations. A highly developed sense of rhythmic flexibility required.

No. 2. L'istesso tempo. (1') T4 M9

When my little dove weeps, I also weep; Mother, let me marry this little maiden.

Key center F-sharp; Aeolian mode. Melody over accompaniment. A rubato section followed by one marked "scherzando, non rubato," although a certain degree of rubato is unavoidable in the latter. Poses the same interpretive difficulties as No. 1.

No. 3. Poco vivo. (45") T6 M5

In October, when the recruits join their regiments, I part from the birds and the trees, and also from the maidens of Csík.

If I climb the rocky mountains, I may find one, maybe two sweethearts; call me fickle if you wish, but she who loved me first will still find me faithful [melody and text of *Eight Hungarian Folksongs*, Sz. 64, No. 5, whose melody is similar to the present example].

Key center F-sharp; Aeolian mode. Staccato ("acuto") melody over arpeggiated accompaniment figures. A keen rhythmic sense needed, especially in view of the awkward and widely spaced left-hand arpeggiations.

Note

1. BBES, p. 273.

Fourteen Bagatelles

Op. 6, Sz. 38
1908
T4-11 M4-11
24' 25"

Publication

Available separately:
B&H

EMB, as *Tizennégy bagatell*

K-BM

Included in:

Balógh, ed. *Bartók. Selected Works for the Piano* (Schirmer).

Chapman, ed. *Béla Bartók. A Highlight Collection of His Best-Loved Original Works* (Maestro).

EMB, publ., *Bartók Album*, Vol. I (Nos. 2, 3, 5, 10, and 14); Vol. II (Nos. 1, 6, 8, and 11); Vol. III (Nos. 4, 7, 9, 12, and 13).

Kail, ed. *Béla Bartók. His Greatest Piano Solos* (Copa).

K-BM, publ., *Bartók. An Album for Piano Solo.*

BBPI, Series I.

Bartók's set of Instructions, prefacing most editions of the *Bagatelles*, offers guidelines for accidentals, pedaling, rests, and tempo indications applicable not only to the present example but to his piano music in general.

Commentary

According to Bartók, this set represents "a new piano style . . . [and] a reaction to the exuberance of the Romantic piano music of the nineteenth century; a style stripped of all unessential decorative elements, deliberately using only the most restricted technical means."[1] In a 1945 lecture, he emphasized that each piece was of one, and only one, tonality and that labels such as "bitonality," "polytonality," or "atonality" did not apply to his music.[2] The set is similar in nature to *Ten Easy Pieces*, Sz. 39, written in the same year, but is technically and interpretively more demanding. It contains the same variety of style and technique as its successor—some pieces based on folk material, some having an etude-like quality, and most being highly experimental and enigmatic. This set should be reserved for the pianist of high intellectual and imaginative capacity.

Movements

The folk texts are excerpted and paraphrased from the English translations in BBHU and BBPI (Series I); complete texts in the original languages appear in BBHU, BBPI (Series I), BBSL (Vol. II) and SODO.

No. 1. Molto sostenuto. (1' 20") T4 M7

Key center C. Two- and three-voice textures. Key signatures of four sharps in the top score and four flats in the bottom score, suggesting bitonality until one discovers the benign C-major cadence at the end. Bartók indicated that "this half-serious, half-jesting procedure was used to demonstrate the absurdity of key signatures in certain kinds of contemporary music."[3] Requires an evasive "tongue-in-cheek" approach.

No. 2. Allegro giocoso. (1' 50") T9 M6

Key center A-flat. Repeated-note motive serving as ostinato in the outer sections and thematic material in the middle section. Good study in staccato and lightness. Some awkward passages involving interlocking hands. Five different accent types. Probably the most popular piece of the set.

No. 3. Andante. (45") T7 M6

Key center C. Chromatic ostinato figure in right hand over left-hand melody. The same awkwardness of interlocking hands as in No. 2. The right-hand part takes on the dimensions of a figural etude, while the left hand must sustain a legato line over long phrase lengths.

No. 4. Grave. (1' 10") T6 M4

> I was a cowherd and I slept by my cows; I awoke in the night and not one beast was in its stall. [The translation in B&H has a different version of the same text and uses the word "kettle" (probably "cattle") in place of "beast."]

Key center D; Aeolian mode. Chordal textures of as many as eight voices, testing one's facility for tonal balance. The texture, or number of voices in a chord, generally fits the dynamic scheme (e.g., eight-voice chord for *ff*, to four-voice chord for *p*). Need for a quick chord rebound technique and sensitivity to extremes of dynamic change.

No. 5. Vivo. (1' 10") T11 M6

> Hey! Before our door, the abandoned young lad, beautiful as a painting, plants a white rose.

Key center G; Dorian mode. Repeated chords of three and four voices over and under folk melody. Two variations and extended coda. Quick shifts in hand position to accommodate the chord changes and endurance in chord playing are absolute essentials. Some three against four counterrhythms.

No. 6. Lento. (1' 35") T4 M7

Key center B. Melody over and under two-voice accompaniment; varied repeats. A study in legato and sustaining accompaniment without aid of pedal. Note offset phrasing in left hand, mm. 12–15. One of the more esoteric of the set.

No. 7. Allegretto molto capriccioso. (2') T9 M11

Key center F-sharp. Freely composed melody under accompaniment of rolled chords alternating with single notes. Frequent tempo changes, some gradual, some sudden, challenging one's sense of timing. The accompaniment is marked staccato throughout and must be maintained with a variety of touches in the left hand. Much awkward interlocking hand activity, which must be under control to convey the sense of abandon and frivolity.

No. 8. Andante sostenuto. (1' 45") T5 M8

Key center G. Plaintive chromatic melodies over grace-note anticipations. Tempo changes and some tricky legato manipulations requiring careful fingering. The mood is one of resigned despair.

No. 9. Allegretto grazioso. (1' 40") T7 M8

Key center E-flat. Continuous melody divided in octaves between the hands. Some angular and tricky rhythmic combinations. Pay particular attention to the differing note values in the "Molto sostenuto" sections, which forecast the last measure ("Largo"), written in *brevis* notation. Pianist must be able to effect sudden contrasts in mood.

No. 10. Allegro. (2' 25") T11 M10

Key center C. A mélange of pianistic figurations, including quick chord changes, legato double-note voicing, dot and wedge staccatos, angular double-note left-hand accompaniment figures, wide leaps, and descending rolled chords. A frenzied atmosphere prevails, as in much of Prokofieff's music.

No. 11. Allegretto molto rubato. (2') T7 M10

Key center A-flat. Descending and ascending scale passages in quartal and tertian harmonies. Tempo changes occur every four to five measures on the average, requiring a keen sense of rubato. Rests occur above certain bar lines, indicating a pause commensurate with the note value (see Bartók's prefatory remarks to the present example).

No. 12. Rubato. (3' 5") T8 M11

Key center B. A mournful and fragmented melody in dotted rhythms prepared by accelerated repeated notes; this material alternates with wavelike scale lines that are more an expressive gesture than a definable melody. Fast repeated notes, frequent changes of meter, fast scale passages requiring unorthodox fingerings, and parallel chords provide the most challenges. This example, along with No. 13, conveys a profound melancholy that contradicts the trifling character that one normally associates with the bagatelle.

No. 13. (Elle est morte [She is dead] - - -). Lento funebre. (1' 45") T6 M8

Key center E-flat. Melody over throbbing (reverse dotted-rhythm) accompaniment. This example and No. 14 are musical reflections of Bartók's ill-fated romance with the violinist Stefi Geyer. Measures 22 and 23 contain a four-note *Leitmotif* in ascending thirds; another treatment of the *Leitmotif* occurs in the "Dedication" to *Ten Easy Pieces*, Sz. 39, and No. 1 of *Elegies*, Sz. 41. The "death" in this instance obviously refers to the relationship between Bartók and Geyer.

No. 14. Valse (Ma mie qui danse [My dancing sweetheart]. . .). Presto. (1' 55") T11 M8

Key center D. Melody over quick waltz patterns in the left hand. The *Leitmotif* occurs periodically throughout the example. According to an article by

Kecskeméti, this finale is of a comically bizarre and macabre nature, similar to that of Liszt's *Mephisto Waltz*, No. 4, entitled "Bagatelle without Tonality."[4] Both examples convey grotesque death images that are portrayed in the tavern scene from Lenau's *Faust*. Need for a nimble left hand and the ability to adjust to changes of meter, counterrhythms, and awkward tertian configuraticns. Brilliant ending. An effective closing piece to a recital or a Bartók group.

Recordings

Hungaroton LPX 12326-33-A, 12333-A. *Bartók at the Piano*, Vol. I, 1981. Side 16, Band 1a (No. 2), 1941.

Vox-Turnabout THS 65010. *Bartók Plays Bartók*. Side 1, Band 2 (No. 2), 1974.

Hungaroton LPX 12334-A. *Bartók Plays and Talks*, Vol. II, 1981. Side 1, Band 2 (No. 10), 1912. Side 1, Band 3a (No. 7), 1912.

The two recordings of No. 2, although made twelve years apart, are quite alike in execution. Both exceed the prescribed MM marking by close to twenty degrees and emphasize a light scherzando approach. The "molto rit." indicated at m. 6 is anticipated in both instances by a full measure, giving an agogic stress to the first and second half notes in the left hand. Lightness and fleeting imagery are also made convincing in Nos. 10 and 7 of the 1912 recordings despite the sound distortion; here again, tempos are faster than Bartók's indicated MM markings.

Notes

1. BBES, p. 432.
2. Ibid., p. 433.
3. Ibid., pp. 432-433.
4. CROW, p. 81.

Ten Easy Piano Pieces

Sz. 39
T2-12 M3-11
16'

Publication

Available separately:
Alfred (Palmer, ed.)

B&H (Nos. 5 and 10 also published separately).

EMB, as *Tíz Könnyü Zongoradarab*

K-BM (No. 10 also published separately).

Maestro (Brimhall, ed.)

MCA

Schott, as *Zehn Leichte Klavierstücke*

Included in:

Agay, ed. *Bartók Is Easy!* (Presser).

Alfred, publ., *Bartók. Twenty-four of his Easiest Piano Pieces.*

Alfred, publ., *Bartók. Twenty-four of his Most Popular Piano Pieces.*

Anson, ed. *Anson Introduces Bartók*, Vols. I and II (Willis).

B&H, publ., *Bartók Album.*

Bradley, publ., *Béla Bartók. Piano Pieces in Their Original Form.*

Brimhall, ed. *My Favorite Bartók* (Hansen, CH II).

EMB, publ., *Bartók Béla. Album*, Vol. I (Nos. 5 and 10), Vol. II (Nos. 3, 7, and 8), Vol. III ("Dedication" and Nos. 2 and 6).

EMB, publ., *Béla Bartók. Young People at the Piano.*

Goldberger, ed. *The Easy Piano Music of Béla Bartók* (Schroeder & Gunther).

Nevin, ed. *Bartók for the Young Pianist* (Pro Art).

Novik, ed. *Young Pianist's Guide to Bartók* (Studio P/R).

Palmer, ed. *Béla Bartók. Selected Children's Pieces for the Piano* (Alfred).

Philipp, ed. *Bartók. 16 Pieces for Children* (International).

BBPI, Series I.

Nos. 3 and 5 transcribed by Károly Vaczi for clarinet (viola) and piano.

The 1945 revision by Bartók introduces guidelines for accidentals, pedaling, rests, and tempo. It is included in BBPI, Series I, p. 105.

Commentary

Bartók intended *Ten Easy Piano Pieces* to be a complementary set to the *Bagatelles*, Sz. 38, but with pedagogical intentions "to supply piano students with easy contemporary pieces."[1] The collection offers a variety of musical styles, while at the same time exemplifying a concentrated idiom that avoids the Romantic excesses of his earlier writing. Not all of them are "easy"; in fact, the levels of difficulty vary considerably from piece to piece (compare the T and M ratings of Nos. 1 and 10). They do however provide a varied musical menu for the piano student and a revealing glance at the many influences the composer was working under at this point in his career.

Movements

The folk texts are excerpted and paraphrased from the English translations in BBHU and BBPI (Series I); complete texts in the original language appear in BBPI (Series I) and SODO.

Dedication. Moderato (1945 edition; no tempo marking in earlier editions). (2' 15") T4 M11

Key center D. An unnumbered introduction to the set. The four-note motive in whole notes at the opening, also found in Nos. 13 and 14 of *Bagatelles*, Sz. 38, represents a *Leitmotif* reflecting Bartók's ill-fated romance with the violinist Stefi Geyer.[2] The *Leitmotif* reappears, fully harmonized, at mm. 30–34. The same sense of stoic despair is found in *Dirges*, Sz. 45. Although technically simple, this selection is hardly a teaching piece for youngsters.

No. 1. Peasant's Song. Allegro moderato. (1') T2 M3

Key center C-sharp; Dorian mode (original edition lacks key signature but 1945 edition has signature of five sharps). Two voices in parallel motion an octave apart. A good basic study in legato, dynamic shading, and execution of three kinds of accents.

No. 2. Painful Struggle (other titles include, "Slow Suffering," "Painful Wrestling"). Lento. (1' 20") T4 M6

Key center D. Two voices in a melody–accompaniment formation. Left-hand ostinato based on the tritone; melody further emphasizes this interval. Suggests the same tormented state of mind as the Chopin Prelude, Op. 28, No. 12.

No. 3. Slovak Young Men's Dance. Allegro. (50") T4 M5

Key center C; Aeolian mode. Melody of four irregular phrase lengths followed by varied repeat mainly in the form of fragmentation. Not a perpetual-motion dance; many dynamic and some tempo gradations, requiring sensitivity along with a keen rhythmic sense. Pay close attention to the subtle differences in touch indications at each cadence (quarter- and eighth-note rhythms).

No. 4. Sostenuto. (1' 20") T4 M8

Key center A. Triadic theme with chromatic embroidery in the accompaniment, framed by a whole-tone scale melody serving as introduction and coda. Much melodic interplay; sonorities that would appeal to the imaginative student. Of the same enigmatic nature as "Dedication."

No. 5. Evening in Transylvania (Evening in the Country). Lento, rubato; Vivo, non rubato. (2' 40") T5 M9

Key centers C and E; pentatonic melodies, Aeolian mode. Original composition, not based on original folk melodies.[3] Five-part form (ABABA), the repetitions subject to variation. Contains splendid textbook examples of the two main types of Hungarian folk music: the free, narrative *parlando-rubato*, or Old Style (A), and the dancelike *tempo giusto*, or New Style (B). The A sections portray vocal melody, the B sections the peasant flute. One of the more popular examples in the set and one frequently performed by Bartók himself.

No. 6. Hungarian Folk Song. Allegretto. (50") T6 M7

> Come, my beloved, to the far end of Ürög's village; I shall rejoice, my love shall weep, and I shall never forget her.

Key center C. Melody built on basically chordal structures of thirds, fifths, and sixths. The inverted dotted rhythm is the most prominent feature of the piece and calls for a bold, sweeping delivery. A good study in double notes for the right hand and offbeat drumlike accompaniment figures in the left.

No. 7. Dawn (Aurora). Molto andante. (1' 30") T5 M9

Key center B. Built mainly on cross-relation thirds and composite harmonic combinations closely related to the style of Debussy. For the extremely sensitive student who is receptive to the possibilities of piano sonority and subtle pedal effects. One of Bartók's finest early-period pieces.

No. 8. Folk Song. Poco andante. (1') T6 M4

> They say: they don't give [Slovakian folk melody (with text in Hungarian) that became the Czechoslovakian national anthem after 1919].

Key center C; Aeolian mode. Three-phrase melody (four, four, and six measures) over sustained chordal accompaniment, parts exchanged. Echo-like two-note slur figure separates the phrases. A study in the tenuto touch used alone and in combination with staccato. The phrase marking of the first four measures obviously applies to all subsequent phrases. Calls for careful dynamic control and quick hand-position shifts over a wide range of the keyboard.

No. 9. Etude (Finger Study). Moderato. (1' 30") T10 M7

Key center A. Modeled after the Clementi and Czerny etudes, but utilizing whole-tone rather than diatonic five-finger positions. Both hands receive equal benefit from the figuration, with expressive legato required in the non-figural hand. Some awkward black-key thumb positions.

No. 10. Bear Dance. Allegro vivace. (1' 45") T12 M5

Key center D. Repeated-note ostinato with chords in parallel motion and accented bass notes. The technical requirements are severe: a quick chord-rebound facility, and speed along with strength in the 4–3–2–1 repetition fingerings. The novice would do well to observe a slower tempo than the indicated

MM marking of quarter note = 120. Much attention should be spent balancing the chords, even at the slower speed.

Recordings

Hungaroton LPX 12326-33. *Bartók at the Piano*, Vol. II, 1981. Side 1, Band 1 (Nos. 5 and 10), 1929; Side 8, Band 1 (No. 5), 1920; Side 15, Band 1 (Nos. 5 and 10), 1945.

Bartók BRS 003 (Nos. 5 and 10), c. 1949/1929.

Welte Legacy of Piano Treasures, Album No. 676 (No. 5), c. 1964/1920.

Vox PLP 6010 (Nos. 5 and 10), c. 1949/1945.

Hungaroton LPX 12334-38. *Bartók Plays and Talks*, Vol. II, 1981. Side 1, Band 1 (No. 10), 1912; Side 1, Band 6 (No. 5), 1922; Side 1, Band 7 (No. 10), 1922.

In No. 5, the A sections in all performances are executed with much rhythmic flexibility, with agogic stresses on the tenutos. The B sections have a light flutelike quality about them and are not lacking in rubato. They begin under tempo and progress to a tempo considerably faster than Bartók's prescribed MM marking of quarter note = 144. In like manner, the tempo of No. 10 is quarter note = 144 in contrast to his indicated high speed of 120. The percussive quality so often associated with the interpretation of this piece is abandoned in favor of a light scherzando approach.

Notes

1. BBES, p. 432.   3. BBES, pp. 349-350.
2. BBLE, p. 384.

Two Elegies

Op. 8b, Sz. 41
No. 1, 1908; No. 2, 1909
T14 M13-14
11' 20"

Publication

Available separately:
B&H

EMB, as *Két Elégia*
K-BM
Included in:
BBPI, Series I.

Several misprints and ambiguities occur in some of the B&H releases: in No. 1, m. 3, the low note in the left hand should read D; m. 42, the second 32d note in the left hand should read D; m. 54, the second octave should read B-flat. In No. 2, m. 9, the first octave in the right hand should read E-flat; m. 59, all left-hand arpeggios should be read in the treble clef.

Commentary

Bartók is said to have referred to this work as "a reversion to the grandiloquence of Romanticism"[1] and a "return to the old style piano technique" similar to that found in No. 4 of the *Sketches*, Sz. 44.[2] Although written in the same year as *For Children*, Sz. 42, the *Elegies* represent, in almost every aspect, the opposite compositional extreme. The simplicity, clarity, and directness of the folksong settings give way in the present example to full massive textures, a virtuosic piano style reminiscent of Liszt and Scriabin, and extreme pathos. Although this diptych represents Bartók's last bastion of Romantic temperament, one finds instances, especially in No. 2, of strikingly progressive compositional techniques that influenced his more advanced style.

Movements

No. 1. Grave. (5' 40") T14 M13
Key center D. Multisectional, free form, much motivic development. This example has been described as "a complaint, a cry of agony," most likely prompted by a letter Bartók had received from the young violinist Stefi Geyer that put an end to their relationship.[3] There are actually occurrences of the Stefi Geyer *Leitmotif* (mm. 19–20, 70–71), which had been made use of in Nos. 13 and 14 of the *Bagatelles*, Op. 6, Sz. 38, and the "Dedication" from *Ten Easy Pieces*, Sz. 39. The technique required is formidable: parallel-octave and full-chordal textures; sweeping arpeggio figures, mostly for the left hand, which span up to five octaves; and random, almost aleatory, 32d-note counterpoint found at mm. 72–85, resembling in some respects the fioritura passages of Chopin and Liszt.

No. 2. Molto adagio, sempre rubato (quasi improvisando). (5' 40") T14 M14
Key center C-sharp. Multisectional, free form, monothematic. In contrast to the lavish emotional exuberance of No. 1, this piece is singularly remarkable

for its economy and thematic unity, despite its having similar textures and as wide a range of expression as its predecessor. Most of the material is derived from a five-note motive (A-sharp, C-sharp, E, G-sharp, A—itself showing some resemblance to the Stefi Geyer *Leitmotif*), which is presented as both accompaniment and thematic material. A significant and far-reaching compositional feature is found in several accompaniment figures of arpeggio and tetrachord figurations for which Bartók provides the following instruction: "the signs o- -o indicate that the accompaniment figures appearing between them need not be fixed in number but may be varied according to the *rubato*, especially in the middle part [m. 30] . . . where the accompaniment should be an even roll."[4] According to Fenyo, "few composers since the period of the *continuo* have permitted the performer [this] freedom of improvisation."[5] It can also be said that this device anticipates "chance" music, which appears later in the century.

Notes

1. BBPI, Series I, p. x.
2. BBES, p. 432.
3. Hungaroton LPX 11335, Vol. III, p. 6.
4. B&H, fn., beginning of No. 2.
5. FENY, p. 85.

For Children

Sz. 42
1908–1909

Publication

Available separately:
Alfred (Palmer, ed.), *Pieces for Children* (1st edition, Vol. I).
B&H (2d edition, Vols. I and II).
B&H (Doflein, ed.), *32 [Easy] Piano Pieces. Béla Bartók* (2d edition, selections from Vols. I and II).
K-BM (1st edition, Vol. I, divided into 2 volumes).
Kjos (Banowetz, ed.) (1st edition, Vol. I).
G. Schirmer (1st edition, Vols. I and II).

UE (2d edition, Vols. I and II, divided into 4 volumes).

Included in:

Agay, ed. *Bartók Is Easy!* (Presser).

Alfred, publ., *Bartók. Twenty-four of his Easiest Piano Pieces.*

Alfred, publ., *Bartók. Twenty-four of his Most Popular Piano Pieces.*

Anson, ed. *Anson Introduces Bartók*, Vols. I and II (Willis).

Bradley, publ., *Béla Bartók. Piano Pieces in Their Original Form.*

Brimhall, ed. *My Favorite Bartók* (Hansen, CH II).

Chapman, ed. *Béla Bartók. A Highlight Collection of His Best-Loved Original Works* (Maestro) (1st edition, Vols. I and II, complete).

EMB, publ., *Béla Bartók. Piano Music for Children.*

Frank, ed. *Bartók. The Best in Music Made Easy for Piano* (Clef).

Goldberger, ed. *The Easy Piano Music of Béla Bartók* (Schroeder & Gunther).

Kail, ed. *Béla Bartók. His Greatest Piano Solos* (Copa). (1st edition, Vols. I and II, complete).

Nevin, ed. *Bartók for the Young Pianist* (Pro Art).

Novik, ed. *Young Pianist's Guide to Bartók* (Studio P/R).

Palmer, ed. *Bartók. An Introduction to His Piano Works* (Alfred).

Philipp, ed. *Bartók. 16 Pieces for Children.*

BBPI, Series II (1st edition, Vols. I and II, complete).

No. 42 transcribed by Bartók for orchestra (No. 5 of *Hungarian Sketches*, Sz. 97, 1931).

Certain selections in *For Children* were revised by the composer in his second edition of 1945. Revisions include the consolidation of the original four-volume series (Rózsnyai, UE) into two volumes; the addition of key signatures; some melodic, harmonic, and metric alterations; augmentation of note values; and the omission of six pieces that had appeared in the 1908–1909 publications.

Denes Agay offers a comparison of the first and second editions in his article "Bartók's For Children, Which Edition? Original? . . . Revised?"[1]

Commentary

The two volumes of *For Children* (85 pieces in all), representing Bartók's first large-scale publication of folk-song transcriptions for piano, is possibly the most attractive collection of its kind in his entire output. Its writing reflects the two activities that were equally dominant at this point in his career: folk music research and piano teaching. His excursions into the peasant villages of Hungary and Slovakia in 1906 harvested an abundance of folk tunes, many of which found their way into the present example. His appointment to the piano chairmanship at the Academy of Music in Budapest prompted an investigation into improved piano teaching techniques, especially for the earlier, more formative years. In a lecture given in 1940, Bartók recalled his intentions:

> This idea originated in my experience as a piano teacher; I had always the feeling that the available material, especially for beginners, has no real musical value, with the exception of very few works—for instance, Bach's easiest pieces, and Schumann's *Jugendalbum*. I thought these works to be insufficient [he most likely meant this in a quantitative sense], and so . . . I myself tried to write some easy piano pieces. At that time the best thing to do would be to use folk tunes. Folk melodies, in general, have great musical value; so, at least the thematical value would be secured. . . .[2]

Although Hungarian and Slovakian folk tunes form the basis for the set, the music itself transcends national boundaries and is presented in a way with which almost every musical level can identify. A variety of teaching pieces provide an abundance of technical and musical challenges for the student, as well as an introduction into the folk modes and scales basic to Bartók's compositional style. No interpretive study of his music is complete without familiarity with this collection.

Movements

Volume I. Hungarian Folk Tunes (first and second editions).
T2-8 M2-6
34' 45"

All titles in Vol. I are Bartók's and originated in the second edition; no titles appear in the first edition.

The folk texts in Vol. I are excerpted and paraphrased from the English translations in Kjos (Banowetz, ed.), BBHU, BBPI (Series II), and personally acquired sources; complete texts in the original language appear in BBHU, BBPI (Series II), and SODO.

No. 1. Children at Play. Allegro. (30") T4 M2

> Let's bake something, I'll tell you what: a snail strudel, round, stuffed, and sweet [children's handkerchief game].

Key center C. Two voices in counterpoint. Differing staccato-slur patterns and dynamic gradations occur simultaneously in both hands. A classic study in touch coordination, not as easy as it looks on the page.

No. 2. Children's Song. Andante. (50") T3 M2

> Come out, sun, for Saint George's day; little lamb on the green nearly dies with cold.

Key center C. Melody with two-voice accompaniment. Slurs and dynamic gradations of differing lengths; the exact value of rests should be carefully observed.

No. 3. Andante ("Quasi adagio" in second edition). (45") T3 M3

I've lost my mate and my lovely marriageable daughter.

Key center A; Dorian mode. Melody with two-voice accompaniment. Two-note slurs on and off the beat. Accents and "smorzando" indication.

No. 4. Pillow Dance. Allegro. (1') T4 M3

I've lost my handkerchief [children's circle dance].

Key center C. Melody over linear accompaniment. Coordination of counterpoint and touches.

No. 5. Play. Poco allegretto; Poco più vivo ("Allegretto; Più mosso" in second edition). (1' 5") T4 M3

Kitty, kitty, have you a pretty girl? [nonsense song].

Key center C. Melody with chordal accompaniment. Echo effects, repeated note patterns, tempo changes, repeat signs, offbeat accompaniment patterns.

No. 6. Study for the Left Hand. Allegro. (50") T5 M3

All these red flowers are like my burning love for you.

Key center D; Aeolian mode. Melody over left-hand ostinato in repeated staccato intervals of varying lengths. A good preliminary study in left-hand wrist flexibility and endurance. Repeated notes in the right hand can be handled just as easily with the third finger instead of the prescribed 2-1-2-1 (first edition) or 4-3-2-1 (second edition). A good recital piece for the indicated level.

No. 7. Play song. Andante grazioso. (30") T3 M3

Go look for the needle! I must mend my love's shirt [circle dance].

Key center C. Melody over chordal accompaniment. Study in offbeat slurs. Pay attention to exact cutoffs in left hand. The bracketed top E in the left hand, m. 12, may be left out if the hand is too small.

No. 8. Children's Game. Allegretto. (1' 30") T4 M5

Give to the poor beggar so that he may go to the town keller. I am a priest, I am an artisan; he who laughs first must forfeit something as a pledge.

Key center A. Dorian and Aeolian modes. Melody over triadic accompaniment. Another study in offbeat slurs and a good variety of touches and accents. Many tempo changes and fermatas suggest quickly changing moods.

No. 9. Song. Adagio; Poco più vivo. (1') T2 M4

White lilies, jump into the Danube; lean on the pitchfork, and rub, wash, and dry yourself well.

Key center D; Ionian and Lydian modes. Melody over two-voice textures. Alternation between meditative and capricious moods, combined with frequently changing dynamics. Requires imagination and sensitivity.

No. 10. Children's Dance. Allegro molto. (40") T5 M3

Lonely people can't be happy [Walachian game].

Key center A; Dorian mode. Melody over left-hand ostinato. Generous pedal markings, which should be strictly observed for the proper effect. A study in accents and dynamic gradations. The F-natural in the left hand, m. 19, is correct but missing in most editions. A brilliant recital piece for the level indicated.

No. 11. Lento. (55") T4 M4

[Same text as No. 3.]

Key center D. Melody over sustained accompaniment in first half, parts exchanged. Note the "espressivo" markings in both parts beginning in m. 13. Fragmentation of second phrase at end suggests a pleading mood.

No. 12. Allegro. (1' 20") T5 M3

Chain, chain, daisy chain [children's play song].

Key center D. Simple melody over accompaniment in thirds. Tempo changes. Left hand takes the melody in the second half, as in No. 11, but presents considerably more coordination and balance difficulties.

No. 13. Ballad. Andante. (30") T4 M4

My horse has run away to the cedar wood; seek not your horse, he's already caught [Mixed Style melody].

Key center D. Melody under sustained right-hand thirds, parts exchanged. Second edition augments note values. A study in the inverted dotted rhythm typical of dramatic folk music (the tune in SODO lacks dotted rhythms and is marked "Rubato"). Influence of Debussy in parallel harmonies in m. 15. Obviously meant as a triptych with Nos. 14 and 15 because of "attacca" ("ad lib.," second edition) indications.

No. 14. Allegretto. (30") T3 M4

> Boys from Rátót stole a goose, but he cackled and gave them away [New Style melody].

Key center D; Dorian mode. Melody with offbeat accompaniment alternating with chordal passages. Second edition augments note values. A study in the *tempo giusto* style and the inverted dotted rhythm.

No. 15. Allegro. (30") T4 M4

> This little girl's frock is too short; sew flounces around it [New Style melody].

> I walk past the house of my beloved on Istvandi Street, but she is still far away from me.

Key center D. Melody with offbeat accompaniment. Frequent tempo and mood changes. A good repeated-note thumb exercise as an alternative to the indicated fingering changes.

No. 16. Old Hungarian Tune. Andante rubato. (30") T3 M5

> I never stole in my whole life, except for six steers [Old Style melody].

Key center A; Aeolian mode. An example of *parlando-rubato*. Second edition indicates phrase separations by way of eighth- and sixteenth-note rests rather than apostrophes (first edition), giving a clearer indication of the pause lengths. A good sense of rhythmic flexibility needed.

No. 17. Round Dance. Adagio ("Lento" in second edition). (1') T3 M3

> My lovely girl is dressed in white; turn to me, you married bride.

Key center E; Aeolian (melodic minor) mode. Melody over swaying accompaniment. Second edition contains augmented note values and more dissonant harmonic effects in mm. 9 and 10. Careful attention to slurring and dynamics needed.

No. 18. Soldier's Song. Andante non molto ("Andante non troppo" in second edition). (1") T3 M4

> At the landing at Nagyvárad stops the steamship; her flag unfurls toward our country, for we old soldiers are going on furlough [New Style melody].

Key center D; Dorian mode. A study in the inverted dotted rhythm often associated with the soldier's song. Second edition contains augmented note values, more dissonant harmonic effects, and a "forte, sonoro" dynamic rather than the "piano, dolce" of the first edition. The same ruggedness of mood as found in No. 13. Obviously meant as a diptych with No. 19 because of the "attacca" ("ad lib.," second edition) indication.

No. 19. Allegretto. (40") T4 M3

> When I go into the inn at Doboz, I'll settle this trifling debt of mine with the hostess and drink some wine [New Style melody].

Key center D; Mixolydian mode. Chordal textures. Second edition augments note values and varies the repeat beginning at m. 9. Indicated finger changes of repeated notes can çause coordination problems; best to maintain basic hand position and repeat the same finger as much as possible.

No. 20. Drinking Song. Poco allegro ("Allegro" in second edition) (25") T4 M3

> The street of Úrógi is straight and you'll not find a pretty maid there; all are hunchbacked and the corners of their mouths are jagged [Old Style melody].

Key center D; mixed modes. Parallel octaves and chords. A rollicking, festive atmosphere that requires brilliance and abandon. Good chord-rebound technique required. Obviously meant as a diptych with No. 21, indicated by the "attacca" ("ad lib." in second edition) indication.

No. 21. Allegro robusto. (20") T5 M3

Key center A; Aeolian mode. Another boisterous drinking song. Chords with offbeat accents. Main difficulty is maintaining balance with melody and offbeat accompaniment in the right hand. Demands good coordination and a keen rhythmic sense.

No. 22. Allegretto (beginning of Vol. 2 in UE). (50") T4 M3

> We want to go to Debrecen to buy a turkey, but must be careful that the turkey does not fall out of the basket.

Key center F. Two-voice counterpoint followed by melody and accompaniment in second part. Requires a light touch and sensitivity to the indicated phrasings and dynamic markings.

No. 23. Allegro grazioso. (50") T5 M3

> Walk this way, that way; Sári and Kati know the way to walk.

Key center C. Melody over linear accompaniment. An awkward left-hand part, where coordination of 3-4-5 fingerings is called for. A variety of touches in the right hand.

No. 24. Andante sostenuto. (50") T4 M3

There's no water in the world like the water from the river Körös.

Key center A; Aeolian mode. Melody over linear accompaniment. A good study in coordination of touches and offbeat slurs. More difficult than it looks on the page.

No. 25. Allegro (left out of second edition). (45") T3 M2

Three apples plus a half; I begged you to be mine, but because you refused, you got what you deserved and bore only daughters.

Key center D. Melody over linear, ostinato accompaniment. Basic study in offbeat slurs of differing lengths. Rhythmic flexibility needed for the transitions.

No. 26. Andante ("Moderato" in second edition). (40") T3 M4

Sweetheart, go around my garden, don't be grief-stricken.

Go away, peacock of the empress; if I were a peacock, I would also get up in the early morning!

Key center G; Aeolian mode. Melody with swaying left-hand accompaniment. First edition presents consistent 3/8 meter, while second edition fluctuates between 3/8 and 2/8. Few pieces in this collection equal the unaffected beauty of this example.

No. 27. Jest. Allegramente. (50") T4 M3

This is what our black gander did: in knee-deep snow he cli-cli-climbed on the goose.

Key center D. Melody with varied accompaniment patterns. Three progressive slower tempo changes require careful proportioning. A crisp, brilliant touch required.

No. 28. Parlando (No. 25 in second edition). (35") T3 M5

László Fehér stole a horse (hej!), but he was caught and put deep into a dungeon.

Key center E; Dorian mode. Melody with sustained chordal accompaniment. Mixed meters. Staccato-tenuto touches. Study in *parlando-rubato* style. The exclamation "Hej!" is coincident with the C-sharp fermatas in the melody.

No. 29. Allegro (left out of second edition). (30") T4 M4

What's this? A bite of stuffed goose for the girls' dinners.

Key center B; Aeolian mode (leading tone at end). Melody over octave doubling, chordal accompaniment, and left-hand counterpoint. Frequent tempo changes.

No. 30. Choral. Andante (No. 28 in second edition). (1' 40") T3 M5

> We've brought in the rooster with his handsome comb; long live the rooster and may he live in peace!

Key center D; Dorian mode. Three variations in chorale style. One of the most beautiful pieces in this collection. Shifting meters, differing touches occur simultaneously in both hands. Influence of Debussy parallelism at m. 33. A good piece for the musically sensitive student.

No. 31. Pentatonic Tune. Allegro scherzando (No. 29 in second edition). (50") T6 M4

> Mother, dear mother, my boots are worn out; who will mend them?

Key center E; Aeolian mode. Octave unisons alternating with two-phrase melodies under offbeat accompaniment. Rapidly changing register shifts requiring some mobility. Grace-note figurations in both hands.

No. 32. Jeering Song. Allegro ironico (No. 30 in second edition). (35") T5 M4

> The sun shines into the church (whoopee!), the priest tolls the bell (whoopee!), enters the church to marry the young couple (whoopee!), and the bride can hardly wait to leave the altar!

Key center C. Melody over repeated-note chordal accompaniments, parts exchanged. The repeated-note chords in the 2/4 measures accompany the shouts of "Ihajja, csuhajja!" (Whoopee!) in the original text. The grace-note accompaniment chords ("Ossia") are difficult but are well worth the effort. Requires good rhythmic sense, the ability to negotiate abrupt dynamic shifts, and a keen sense of humor.

No. 33. Andante sostenuto (No. 31, "Andante tranquillo" in second edition). (1' 30") T4 M6

> Stars shine brightly to help the poor chap find his beloved's house [New Style melody].

> Wherever I go, even the trees are weeping [text incomplete].

Key center F; Aeolian mode. Two-voice counterpoint with occasional left-hand chords. Second edition contains augmented note values. A fine example of the way Bartók provides articulation markings to replace dynamic markings (e.g., at the very opening melodic statement, light portato touch indications progress to heavier, more sustained tenuto-staccato and finally tenuto indications, suggesting a crescendo); the diminuendo signs are left out of the second edition. Obviously meant as a diptych with No. 34 because of "attacca ad libitum" indication. This piece should be reserved for the most musically sensitive student with a refined sense of tone.

No. 34. Andante (No. 32 in second edition). (1' 15") T5 M4

> When my ox is finished eating the after-grass, I'll tie him up and then go to my sweetheart who awaits me [Old Style melody].

> Oh, lovely white flower, come during the evening so that I can look into your eyes.

Key center F; Aeolian mode. Melody with widely spaced left-hand intervals in the accompaniment. Good for developing tactile sense in the left hand. Tricky rhythmic patterns of inverted dotted rhythms and offbeat accompaniment patterns.

No. 35. Allegro non troppo (No. 33 in second edition). (45") T5 M4

> I picked some flowers in my garden and hurt my feet; it is good that God did not let me marry!

Key center A; Aeolian mode. A companion piece to No. 34 in developing left-hand tactile sense with jump-bass patterns. Also offers a variety of touches, offbeat slurs, and accents.

No. 36. Allegretto (No. 34 in second edition). (30") T4 M4

> Alas, how beautifully falls the rain and how beautifully green is the field and my grazing flock; my beloved, alas, is soldiering [New Style melody].

Key center G; Aeolian mode (raised seventh). Melody in parallel thirds, fourths, and first-inversion triads. Meter in first edition is 2/4, 4/4 in second edition, but the note values are the same, suggesting longer phrase lengths; also, the "cresc.-dim." signs are left out of the second edition. Good study in parallel chords and intervals. Obviously meant as a triptych with Nos. 37 and 38 because of "attacca" ("ad lib.," second edition) indications.

No. 37. Poco vivace (No. 35, "Con moto" in second edition). (25") T4 M4

> In the high forest around Kisdoboz is a gold-brown maiden; if I could be the farthest tree in this forest, I would rest upon my love's shoulder! [New Style melody].

> The golden-feathered peacock is beautiful; but once his feathers are made muddy by the foamy water of Maros, I will be with my darling.

Key center G; Dorian and Aeolian modes. Melody with chords and jump bass. Lavish harmonies reminiscent of some of Brahms's Hungarian rhapsodies. Mixed meters and moods.

No. 38. Drunkard's Song. Allegro (No. 36, "Vivace in second edition). (35")
T6 M4

> Beyond the Danube a little suckling pig is cooking on a fire of oak and a spit of
> beech; come, sweetheart, to bed [Mixed Style melody].
>
> Ten liters of wine are in me; I am well dressed and in high spirits!

Key center G; Dorian and Aeolian modes. Four-part chorale style. Some
sobering difficulties in rhythmic coordination (mm. 1 and 2). Requires quick
chord-rebound facility and a feeling of reckless abandon.

No. 39. Swine-Herd's Song. Allegro (No. 37 in second edition). (35") T6
M4

> Swineherd of Csór, what are you cooking?
> Lights [pork lungs] with cabbage cooked in fat.
> Make the old man eat it or hit him on the cheek [Mixed Style melody].
>
> The cricket marries the gnat's daughter; the louse wants to give the bride away;
> the flea wants to be best man; all kinds of smelly bugs want to be guests.

Key center G; Aeolian mode. Four phrases of equal length with varied
repeat. Melody over counterpoint, parts exchanged. Downbeat and offbeat
slurs, a variety of accents, parallel thirds. Need to pay close attention to the
subtle dynamic changes and to create a bright, festive atmosphere throughout.
This text suggests a dialogue-type interpretation, where voices are exchanged
every two measures.

No. 40. Winter Solstice Song. Allegro (No. 38 in second edition). (35") T6
M4

> May the Lord give two little oxen to the head of this household; He has also
> granted him a magic formula [carol for the Christmas season].

Key center F. Four variations and coda. Melody over a descending-
tetrachord ostinato pattern. Long-range dynamic changes need careful gauging. Variety of accent markings suggest very subtle phrasing and unwritten
dynamic changes. One of the most technically intricate of the set.

No. 41. Allegro moderato (No. 39 in second edition). (1' 35") T5 M6

> Are you going away and leaving me, my love?
> Oh yes, I am indeed.
> If you leave, I will too.
> Well then, let's go away together [Old Style melody].

Key center D minor. Unison melody stated in left hand followed by four
variations with varying moods and tempos corresponding to the dialogue in the

text. For the sensitive and musically mature student. Study of the text and its relationship to the Bartók setting is essential.

No. 42. Swine-Herd's Dance. Allegro vivace (No. 40 in second edition). (1' 45") T8 M5
Variant of No. 39 (first edition); the tune was also played on the *furulya*, a wooden peasant flute.

Key center G; Mixolydian mode. Introduction, four variations, and coda. Melody undergoes alteration in the variations and fragmentation in the outer sections. A variety of ostinato accompaniments. A splendidly conceived dynamic arch form covers the entire piece (*pp–ff–pppp*). Requires careful gauging of long-range dynamic changes and technical control of a variety of touches. A virtuoso piece that can successfully end a group of selections from this collection or a miscellaneous Bartók group.

Volume II. Slovakian Folk Tunes (beginning of Vol. 3 in UE).
T3–7 M3–8
34' 40"

Slovakia, a region in eastern Czechoslovakia, was part of Hungary at the time of writing of the first edition. Musical and stylistic differences between the two volumes are practically imperceptible; the languages of the original folk texts seem to be the only distinguishing features.

All titles in Vol. II are Bartók's own, although some changed between the first and the second edition.

The folk texts in Vol. II are excerpted and paraphrased from the English translations in BBPI (Series II) and personally acquired sources; complete texts in the original language appear in BBPI (Series II), BBSL (Vols. I and II), and SODO.

No. 1. Allegro. (30") T4 M2

> If there were cherries, every Slovak girl would be proud; if roses and lilies would bloom, the queen would get a husband.

Key center F. Melody with broken-chord accompaniment. Main difficulty is in the coordination of non-coincident slurs and stresses. The Alberti accompaniment usually starts on the third of the triad, further compounding the difficulties. Obviously meant as a triptych with Nos. 2 and 3 because of "attaca" ("ad lib.," second edition) indications.

No. 2. Andante. (45") T4 M3

> Kite settled on the branch, I look at the river and often gazed after you, O lad.

Key center F. Left-hand melody surrounded by jump-bass accompaniment in the right hand. Good for developing hand-over-hand facility and tonal balance in favor of the left hand.

No. 3. Allegretto. (30") T3 M3

> That girl gave me one of two roses by the tree; give me the other one, because it means love; I won't give it, because there'll be none left for me.

Key center F. Melody with offbeat accompaniment. A teasing, scherzando approach needed. Syncopated accents and a variety of touches.

No. 4. Wedding Song. Andante. (30") T3 M4

> Hey, Lado, Lado; for whom are you sewing, Mummy? For you, my daughter, for you are leaving me.

Key center F. Two-voice counterpoint. Sparse texture, shifting meter, and dissolute ending suggest a melancholy, reticent mood for this short piece.

No. 5. Variations. Molto andante. (2' 15") T4 M4

> The peacock flew to his mother; play merrily, musicians, for my bridal wreath and golden ring are on the wall.

Key center G; Lydian mode. Four variations. Two-voice counterpoint in theme and variation 2; chordal textures in the relative minor in variation 3; rhythmic diminution suggests a more joyous mood in variation 4. Bright, fresh harmonies and direct sentiments make this piece unusually appealing.

No. 6. Rondo (first edition); Round Dance I (second edition). Allegro. (40") T5 M3

> There is an old witch, she has three sons; one goes to school, one sews slippers, and one sits on a rock playing a bagpipe.

Key center C; Ionian mode with hints of Lydian in the accompaniment. Melody with a variety of single-voice accompaniment patterns. A challenge in coordination of two-voice counterpoint and offbeat slurs, much like No. 1 of Vol. I, but at a faster tempo.

No. 7. Rogue's Song (first edition); Sorrow (second edition). Andante. (50") T3 M4

> The sheriff wanted to hang me, but there were girls there who did not allow it.

Key center A; composite modes. Melody with legato accompaniment becoming syncopated at repetition. A popular piece with direct appeal. Can be used as a rudimentary study in legato and slur combinations.

No. 8. Dance Song (first edition); Dance (second edition). Allegro ("non trop-po," second edition). (35") T5 M3

> Two pigeons in love sit on the tower of Presov; people are watching them with envy.

Key center E; Aeolian mode. Melody over rhythmic ostinato in chords. Good coordination facility and keen rhythmic sense needed. Lively and brilliant, immediately appealing.

No. 9. Children's Song (first edition); Round Dance II (second edition). Andante. (30") T3 M4

> Unfold yourself, blossom, you green shrubs of the island.

Key center B-flat; Lydian mode at cadence points. A graceful, lilting melody over simple accompaniment. A delicate temperament can easily identify with this short piece.

No. 10. Mourning Song (first edition); Funeral Song (second edition). Largo. (1' 10") T3 M4

> In the barracks of Mikulas, my dead lover is laid out.

Key center A; Aeolian mode. Melody over undulating tetrachord accompaniment. Incongruous dynamic schemes occur between the hands. Sensitivity needed.

No. 11. Lento. (1") T3 M4

> On the field of Bystrov three roses are blooming; hoya boy! You gave your fragrance to me for three years, O my God!

Key center D; Dorian mode. Left-hand melody with right-hand accompaniment; reverse procedure in variation 1. Second edition augments note values. A good sight-reading study in metric values. Obviously meant as a triptych with Nos. 12 and 13 because of "attaca" ("ad lib.," second edition) indication.

No. 12. Poco andante (first edition); Andante rubato (second edition). (40") T3 M5

> Mother of my lover, whichever way I go, don't curse my path.

Key center G; Dorian mode. Melody with two-voice contrapuntal accompaniment. Tempo and dynamic changes occur with rapid frequency. A study in minute detail of expression.

No. 13. Allegro. (40") T5 M3

I went into the water to fetch the straying geese and my shirt got wet; when I go to my sweetheart, it will be better.

Key center G; mixture of Dorian and Aeolian modes. Two-voice counterpoint. A study in touch coordination and the concept of slurring over rests. Fresh, appealing harmonies.

No. 14. Moderato. (35") T3 M6

On the pine-topped hill, four oxen are plowing, two harrowing; who is driving them?

Key center D; mixed modes. Melody with chordal accompaniment. A miniature study in *parlando-rubato* and *tempo giusto* styles, which alternate in close succession. A surprisingly abundant variety of touches in this short piece.

No. 15. Bagpipe Tune (first edition); Bagpipe (second edition). Molto tranquillo. (55") T4 M4

Dance, maiden, dance, till your boots are tattered; your darling is a cobbler and he will mend them for you.

Key center G. Left-hand melody with right-hand offbeat accompaniment; reverse procedure in variations 2 and 3. The "forte" and "pesante" indications are curiously contradictory to the opening tempo indication. Perhaps the message is that loud and heavy touches need to be modified in favor of a more cantabile delivery.

No. 16. Lament. Lento. (50") T3 M6

[Text unfit to print.]

Key center E; Aeolian mode. Melody with two-voice counterpoint. Short study in rubato and subtle changes in mood. Second edition augments note values. Repeated-note fingering 1-3-2 in first edition judiciously changed to 2-2-2 in second edition. Obviously meant as a diptych with No. 17 because of "attaca" ("ad lib.," second edition) indication.

No. 17. Andante. (45") T4 M5

The orphan girl was the priest's maidservant; she slew eleven of the robbers who were sleeping in the tower, and left Janko alive for herself.

Key center D; Aeolian mode. Melody with two-voice accompaniment. A study in irregular phrasing. Colorful pedal effects beginning at m. 14.

No. 18. Jeering Song (first edition); Teasing Song (second edition). Sostenuto-Allegro vivace. (35") T6 M4

Once I was your lover, now I am your comrade, but who cares? If I go out to the street, I will find an ape better than you; I don't need you!

Key center E. Left-hand melody with offbeat accompaniment; reverse procedure in second verse. Coordination problems and quick adjustments needed in balance and dynamics.

No. 19. Romance. Assai lento. (1' 25") T3 M4

Bird on the sorrowful branch, my lover is far away, far away.

Key center A; Aeolian mode with alterations. Two-voice counterpoint with cadential chord progressions for the text repetitions (as in "far away"). Use of separating signs. A study in legato and tone production at different dynamics.

No. 20. Frisky (first edition). Prestissimo. Game of Tag (second edition). Presto. (25") T5 M3

Don't go at dawn, Hanulienka, to the thorny bush, because your flounced skirt will get torn there.

Key center F; Lydian mode. Melody with broken-chord accompaniment. Pure white-key music, no accidentals. Awkward left-hand figurations.

No. 21. Funny Story (first edition); Pleasantry (second edition). Allegro moderato. (1') T5 M4

She flew down and was in tears that she did not get fed [sixteen verses, some unfit to print].

Key center C. Left-hand melody with offbeat accompaniment in right hand; reverse procedure in second verse. The repeated notes at mm. 3 and 7 correspond to the exclamatory refrain "aj jaj" of the original text. Needs control of simultaneous dynamic and tempo changes, mm. 29–42.

No. 22. Revelry. Molto allegro. (50") T6 M4

The lads caught a goat, they found him in the forest: I will go there to ask them whether my darling is well.

Key center A; Aeolian mode with alterations. Melody repeated on different pitch levels over ostinato-type accompaniment. Excellent left-hand study utilizing all five fingers in different interval combinations. Attention to detail a must.

No. 23. Molto rubato, non troppo lento (left out of second edition; beginning of Vol. 4 in UE). (2' 40") T4 M6

I am already an old shepherd, I shall not live till spring; none of the birds of spring will wake me.

Key center D; Dorian mode with raised fourth. Melody with pulsating accompaniment with harmonic variants in each of the four verses. Any rubato should be restricted to the right-hand melody, with the left-hand rhythms clearly defined. Some exquisite color combinations possible with judicious use of pedal. Obviously meant as a triptych with Nos. 24 and 25 because of "attaca (ad libitum)" indication.

No. 24. Poco andante. (No. 23, "Andante tranquillo" in second edition). (40") T3 M5

> I passed through the pine forest, and stepped on a cold stone; under the stone is a well which Zuzička drank from.

Key center D; Dorian and Aeolian modes. Melody with offbeat accompaniment. A study in the inverted dotted rhythm, which is relatively uncommon in this volume. Almost every measure sees a tempo or dynamic change of one kind or another, requiring flexibility of musical concept.

No. 25. Andante. (No. 24 in second edition). (50") T4 M5

> Wide stream, quickly flowing; my beloved, bring my horse some water.

Key center A; Aeolian mode. Melody alternating with linear accompaniment. Careful attention to full duration of ties in the left hand; the fan-out harmonic effects are very effective.

No. 26. Scherzando. (No. 25 in second edition). Allegretto. (45") T5 M4

> It is already evening, it is dark; my love is not yet at home. My God! Who will embrace me this evening?

Key center G; Mixolydian mode. Melody with two-voice accompaniment. Good study in right-hand leggiero and left-hand legato suspensions. Some clever harmonic effects, which need sensitive attention.

No. 27. Jeering Song (left out of second edition). Allegro. (35") T7 M4

> Hey! To which family belongs the girl standing on the hill? Perhaps she has a headache [I-ha-ja] or doesn't want to work [Ša-la-ja].

Key center F; Aeolian mode. Octave unisons combined with chords. Some very tricky left-hand chordal slurs in the middle section, requiring quick chordal adjustments.

No. 28. Shepherd's Flute (first edition). Peasant's Flute (No. 26 in second edition). Andante molto rubato. (1') T4 M6

> [Music for the *fujera*, or wooden peasant flute.]

Key center E; Mixolydian mode. Difficult rhythmic combinations, tempo changes, and rubato effects challenge one's sense of timing. Changes of mood. Pleasing harmonic effects.

No. 29. Another Joke (first edition); Pleasantry II (No. 27 in second edition). Allegro. (50") T7 M5

The drake sits in the valley [text incomplete].

Key center A. Melody over broken-chord accompaniment. A difficult left hand with melodic implications in the double stemming. Awkward leaps in both hands, mm. 14-16. The ritards in the introductory measures to each variation require a keen sense of timing along with a feeling of abandon.

No. 30. Lament (No. 28 in second edition). Andante, molto rubato. (55") T3 M5

I have wandered many nights on bumpy, cold and muddy roads; but I never minded them, for I spent the nights with girls.

Key center G; non-diatonic mode, augmented second between third and fourth scale degrees. Melody over sustained chords and broken chords. Good study in rubato (both left and right hands) and irregular phrasings.

No. 31. Canon (No. 29 in second edition). Poco vivace (first edition); Allegro non troppo (second edition). (50") T6 M4

Sleep, sleep, I would sleep [text.incomplete].

Key center E; Aeolian mode. Canonic imitation at the octave with repeated chords and intervals. Good study in chord-rebound and parallel-third techniques. Pedal effects. Changes of tempo and mood.

No. 32. Bagpipe Tune (first edition); Bagpipe (No. 30 in second edition). Vivace. (55") T6 M3

Lettuce grows in the little garden: my darling Janiček, let us love each other, my mother doesn't care.

Key center G; Ionian mode. Melody over drone-type accompaniment. Severe coordination problems in the left hand need individual attention before the two hands are combined. Style straightforward and transparent.

No. 33. The Orphan (left out of second edition). Poco Andante. (1' 20") T4 M5

Hey, green forest, your pain fills my head; my parents have died long ago, leaving me an orphan.

Key center D; Dorian mode. Melody over linear accompaniment stated three times in sequence. This example and No. 34 were composed by Emma Gruber Sándor, wife of Zoltán Kodály. The three melodic statements adhere closely to the moods of the text by way of dynamic and tempo changes.

No. 34. Romance (left out of second edition). Poco allegretto. (1' 15") T5 M5

I know a little forest; in the little forest is a little house.

Key center G; Dorian mode. Melody with introduction and accompaniment in rising and falling fifths similar to the tuning of a string instrument; these accompaniment figures should remain in the left hand for proper balance. Offbeat accompaniments in right hand over second melodic statement. Frequent tempo changes. Surprise ending. A wistful mood should be maintained throughout.

No. 35. Highwayman's Tune (first edition); The Highway Robber (No. 31 in second edition). Allegro. (40") T4 M4

Janosik is a big bully; he would have beaten me sorely, but he left his belt home on the table.

Key center F. Melody with counterpoint and drone accompaniment in fifths. Bold beginning followed by two melodic statements of increasing docility. Good study in mood changes corresponding with the text.

No. 36. Largo (first edition); Pesante (No. 32 in second edition). (55") T4 M5

If I knew where my darling mows hay in the morning, I would bring him roses in my apron.

Key center C; non-diatonic mode (major with lowered sixth). Key signature A-flat (!). Melody with linear and fragmented accompaniment. Augmented note values in second edition. Inverted dotted rhythms. The delicate texture seems to contradict the "pesante" indication of the second edition; care should be taken to keep the dynamic within appropriate limits. A good sight-reading "game" because of the hidden key signature.

No. 37. Molto tranquillo (first edition); Andante tranquillo (No. 33 in second edition). (45") T4 M4

The Danube's bank is green at Bratislava [lament about a soldier who has had to leave his lover].

Key center C; Aeolian mode. Melody over rolled-chord and linear accompaniment. Note values augmented in second edition. Another example of the

inverted dotted rhythm, but requiring delicacy rather than boldness of statement. A piece of unpretentious beauty.

No. 38. Farewell (No. 34 in second edition). Adagio. (1' 35") T5 M6

> I look back upon you once more, mountain of Zvolen; I would like to speak to
> you once more, my darling.

Key center D; Aeolian mode. Left-hand melody under suspended chords.
A hauntingly beautiful and sensitively conceived example. Performer needs to
keep the accompaniment in the background at all times and to pay particular
attention to dynamic shadings that occur there. Good study in rhythmic
precision for the lower voice.

No. 39. Ballad (No. 35 in second edition). Poco largo—Allegro (first edition);
Moderato—Allegro (second edition). (1' 30") T5 M7

> Janko drives out two oxen [sad tale of a farmer who is killed by highway robbers
> because of his refusal to give up his possessions and their refusal to bargain].

Key center D; Aeolian mode. Melody in various registers and accompaniments through five variations and coda. Many changes in tempo and mood to
correspond with the story line. The different fingerings given for the repeated
notes in the principal theme—(1 + 2)-(1 + 2)-(1 + 2)-(1 + 2); 3-3-3-3; 2-1-2-
1; and 4-3-2-1—seem to suggest an increasing lightness of touch. Sensitivity
to the narrative quality of this example required.

Nos. 40 and 41. Rhapsody (Nos. 36 and 37 in second edition). Parlando,
molto rubato—Allegro moderato. (2' 5") T7 M6

> Hey, blow you summer wind; clouds, wet the ground with dew; hey, green forest,
> if you saw my darling, you would bring her to me! [No. 40].

> Hey, what a beautiful house is this county hall; Janko, will you sit here some day?
> Janiček Vršovský, don't go without your axe! I have no fear alone; if seven would
> come, or even twelve, I will thrash my way out of it! [No. 41].

Key center G; Lydian mode (No. 41), with alternating statements (No. 40)
in various key centers and modes. Form A B A'B'A"B" going through respec-
tive key centers of G, G, B, D, F, and G. Study in contrasts between *parlando-
rubato* and *tempo giusto* styles. A prototype in miniature of the Hungarian
rhapsodies of Liszt, but making use of peasant rather than Gypsy folk material.
A variety of touches and slurrings are found in each statement of the themes,
suggesting differing moods and dynamics.

No. 42. Mourning Song (first edition); Dirge (No. 38 in second edition).
Lento. (1' 30") T4 M6

Hey, Mountain, little green mountain; hey, who will love my rosy cheeks tonight?

Key center G; Phrygian mode with raised third. Left-hand melody under sustained two-voice textures. This example and No. 43 represent a style of writing uncharacteristic of the other examples in *For Children*, but similar to the more enigmatic examples in *Bagatelles*, Sz. 38, and *Dirges*, Sz. 45. Good study in tonal balance favoring the left hand, and double-note legato in the right hand.

No. 43. Funeral Song (first edition); Mourning Song (No. 39 in second edition). Lento. (2' 5") T4 M8

There in the deep valley, my dear father lies under the black earth; he will never ask me, "Hey, how are you, my servant?"

Key center E; Dorian mode. Three melodic statements interspersed with a haunting motive in dotted rhythm. An intense, mournful example of *parlando-rubato* style. Each of the three melodic statements offers different phrasings and stress markings, in similar fashion to certain examples in *Improvisations*, Op. 20, Sz. 74. This final piece of the collection is probably the most difficult interpretively and the most indicative of Bartók's more mature style of folk arrangement for piano.

Recordings

Hungaroton LPX 12333-A. *Bartók at the Piano*, Vol. I, 1981. Side 15, Band 2 (Vol. I, Nos. 3, 4, 6, 10, and 12), 1945; Side 15, Band 3 (Vol. I, Nos. 13, 15, 18, 19, and 21), 1945; Side 15, Band 4 (Vol. I, Nos. 26, 34, 35, 31, and 30), 1945.

Vox PLP 6010, c. l949/1945.

Hungaroton LPX 12334-A. *Bartók Plays and Talks*, Hungaroton Bartók Record Archives, Vol. II. Side 1, Band 3 (Vol. II, No. 10), 1912.

The 1945 recordings are significant in that they are probably the last piano recordings Bartók ever made, some eight months before his death. Much of the performance betrays a ponderousness and melancholy contrary to the fresh and buoyant naïveté of most of these pieces. The "f, molto marcato" of No. 6 gives way to an interpretation that is quite benign; the tempo seems quite slow in No. 10, but is in keeping with Bartók's MM indication of quarter note = 160 in the second edition of the same year. Both the 1912 and the 1945 recordings of this piece corroborate the F-natural in the left hand, m. 19, which is not indicated in the second edition. Some octave doublings occur in Nos. 15 (right hand), 18 (left hand, beginning in m. 7), 19 (right hand, beginning in m. 9), and 21 (left hand, beginning in m. 1; right hand, beginning in m. 17), suggesting an alternative version for concert use. Also in No. 21, the marcato slur tones found in mm. 5–7 are agogically accented to the point of sounding like triplet eighth and sixteenth rhythms, a mannerism that occurs frequently in Bartók's playing.

Notes

1. *Clavier*, March 1971, 18–23.   2. BBES, p. 426.

Two Romanian Dances

Op. 8a, Sz. 43
No. 1, 1909; No. 2, 1910
T12–13 M11
8' 30"

Publication

Available separately:
B&H
G. Schirmer (Delius, ed.)
EMB, as *Két román tánc*
K-BM

Included in:
Balógh, ed. *Bartók. Selected Works for the Piano* (Schirmer).
K-BM, publ., *Bartók. An Album for Piano Solo*.
BBPI, Series I.

No. 1 transcribed for orchestra by Bartók (*Romanian Dance*, 1910); and by Leo Weiner (1939).

   A facsimile reproduction (SORO), published by EMB in 1974 with commentary by László Somfai, makes comparisons with manuscripts and early editions. This study is very important in view of discrepancies in certain editions, some still in print (compare the octave vs. single-note melodic settings of mm. 64–71 of No. 1 in K-BM, G. Schirmer, and BBPI).

Commentary

This set, the first by Bartók for piano based on Romanian folk music, reflects the vigor and exuberance characteristic of the Romanian folk dance. Although Bartók asserts that the movements are "based on original thematic material and not on folk tunes,"[1] Suchoff takes exception to this claim (see No. 2). Three elements of Romanian folk music are incorporated in the present examples: the continuous variation of an instrumental melody; a four-line melodic structure in duple meter with variations; and the use of an accented tritone above the closing or central note of the melody. Either piece can be performed on its own or can effectively end a recital or a Bartók group.

Movements

No. 1. Allegro vivace. (4' 30") T12 M11

[Unrelated to a specific folk tune, "but of a completely Romanian character."[2]]

Key center C; Phrygian mode. ABA form; almost all materials represent developmental treatment of the opening material, which features the two six-teenth notes and an eighth rhythmic motive. Almost the entire piece is based on four-measure phrase lengths, which constantly increase in texture and intensity, relieved only by the section starting in m. 64 marked "Lento." In keeping with Bartók's final intentions, the first melodic statement of this section should be played in octaves and the second (m. 67) in single notes at the upper octave. Clarity and careful articulation are needed in this example in particular, especially when melodic activity occurs in the lower registers. It is also important to observe the precise pedal indications and to avoid too massive a sound effect in the climactic sections. One of the first examples of virtuoso treatment of the folk element in Bartók's piano works, this piece will appeal to the college-level student with good technical equipment and rhythmic sense.

No. 2. Poco Allegro. (4') T13 M11

Women have a weak mind, but the men's is weaker still, for it goes about un-girdled [jeering song, according to Suchoff[3]].

Key center G; mixed modes. Broken octaves used as an ostinato figure for the introductory theme (m. 3) and for the theme proper (m. 16); these two materials alternate throughout the piece and are extensively developed. Four-measure structures similar to those of No. 1. Short-range and sudden dynamic contrasts. Awkward technical situations, involving interlocking hand positions, parallel sixths in the left hand, quick octave and chordal leaps, grace notes, and three-note trills. Comparable to No. 1 in virtuosity, but not as often played and more difficult to make convincing.

Recordings

Hungaroton LPX 12326-A. *Bartók at the Piano*, Vol. I, 1981. Side 1, Band 2 (No. 1), 1929.

Bartók BRS 003 (No. 1), c. 1949/1929.

Hungaroton LPX 12334-A. *Bartók Plays and Talks*, Vol. II, 1981.

Regarding the 1929 recording, Somfai suggests that we "exercise some care in accepting the tempos in the surprisingly fast and virtuoso performance—for it is true that pieces which he played often did frequently become faster in Bartók's performance, but he was also possibly urged on by the limited time available for one record-side at that stage."[4]

Despite the fast tempi (quarter note = c. 176 vs. the indicated 160), one experiences an extraordinarily compelling rhythmic drive and vitality in these performances. There is the strange feeling at the repeat of the first phrase at m. 7 that the performer has "shifted" into higher gear, although there is no perceptible tempo change. Light pedals are used on the downbeats beginning in m. 16. In both performances of the "Lento" section, Bartók chooses to take octaves on the first strain and single notes on the repetition, producing somewhat of an echo effect (this distribution is found in K-BM). At the climactic section ("Tempo I," beginning in m. 97), there is a wonderful feeling of grandeur without any loss of the rhythmic momentum or the dancelike quality preceding it. At the last two measures of the piece, Bartók does not attempt to "clean out" the sonority, as would seem to be indicated in the notation and pedal markings, but lets the octaves in the upper staff sustain and blend in with the final chord, providing a more conclusive effect for the performer.

Notes

1. BBES, p. 432.
2. Ibid.
3. BBPI, Series I, p. xii. Complete text and English translation appear in BBPI, Series I, and BBRO, Vol. II.
4. SORO, p. 27.

Seven Sketches

Op. 9b, Sz. 44
1908-1910
T4-12 M4-11
11' 30"

Publication

Available separately:
EMB, as *Vázlatok*
K-BM
B&H
Marks (erroneously classified as Op. 9)

Included in:
Balógh, ed. *Bartók. Selected Works for the Piano* (Schirmer).
EMB, publ., *Bartók Album*, Vol. I (Nos. 1, 2, 5, and 6); Vol. II (No. 7); Vol. III (Nos. 3 and 4).
K-BM, publ., *Bartók. An Album for Piano Solo*.
BBPI, Series II.

Also entitled *Esquisses* in some references, probably borrowed from the work of the same name by Debussy.

The 1945 revision by Bartók contains introductory commentary pertaining to his editorial changes (found only in No. 4, mm. 37-40) and the tonality of some of the pieces: "Sketch 4—C-sharp minor, Sketch 7—B major. This information is addressed especially to those who like to pigeonhole all music they do not understand into the category of 'atonal' music."[1]

Commentary

According to Bartók, the *Sketches* "represent, on the whole, a similar trend as observed in the *Bagatelles* [Sz. 38], although in Sketch No. 4 there is a certain return to the old style piano technique (note the 'decorative' broken chords there and similar effects in the *Elegies* [Sz. 41])."[2] Like the *Bagatelles* and *Ten Easy Pieces*, Sz. 39, the *Sketches* offer a wide variety of musical styles and influences that the composer was working under at this point in his career. With the exception of Nos. 4 and 7, they are not excessively difficult, but do require a large hand capable of blocking or stretching tenths.

Movements

No. 1. Portrait of a Girl. Andante (con moto). (1' 40") T6 M9

Key center G. Four-part form built around a short rhythmic motive (dotted or triplet rhythm leading to sustained tone) that undergoes extensive melodic and harmonic variation. A very attractive piece, dedicated to Bartók's first wife, Márta Ziegler. Frequent tempo and dynamic changes. Expression markings alternating between "semplice" and "espressivo" require a flexible interpretive sense. Large left-hand reaches, including some five-note chords.

No. 2. See-Saw, Dickory-Daw. Commodo. (50") T4 M4

Key center C. Two voices in parallel motion and counterpoint. Like No. 1 of the *Bagatelles*, this piece appears to be bitonal, although the final cadence reveals it to be "undisputably a pure C major."[3] Requires lightness of touch and childlike abandon.

No. 3. Lento. (1' 50") T6 M9

Key center C. Fragmentary motives over accompaniment mainly in tenths. A meditative piece dedicated to Emma and Zoltán Kodály on the occasion of their wedding (August 1910). For best effect, the tones in the left hand should be sustained manually without aid of the pedal. Needs a good sense of metric pulse and the ability to adjust to frequent rhythmic and tempo changes.

No. 4. Non troppo lento. (3' 40") T12 M11

Key center C-sharp. The most difficult piece of the set, similar in nature to the *Elegies* and "built on a close association of bitonality, construction of thirds, pentatony and whole tones."[4] Parallel seventh chords, trills, sweeping arpeggio figures, and quasi-glissando figurations all come into play with no thematic tie-in other than an inverted dotted rhythm, which permeates the piece. A difficult piece to make convincing.

No. 5. Romanian Folk Melody. Andante rubato. (1' 10") T7 M8

> Everybody cared for me, only sense I did not have; my silly mind made a servant out of me.[5]

Key center B. Melody in octaves over widely spaced left-hand chords. Requires a good legato octave technique in the right hand, a large reach and a nimble rolled-chord facility in the left, and vigilant adherence to the frequent tempo changes.

No. 6. In Walachian Style. Allegretto. (35") T4 M4

"Original thematic material, but of completely Rumanian character."[6]

Key center E. Four-phrase melody in octave doubling, fragmented upon its repetition. Offbeat slurs and five-finger patterns in a quasi-glissando style. The main difficulty is the articulation of moving voices along with sustained tones.

No. 7. Poco lento. (1' 45") T7 M10
Key center B. Triadic melody, presented singularly, in imitation, and in octave doubling, undergoes a developmental process resulting in pentachordal patterns of two whole-tone scales played simultaneously. Similar patterns are found at the end of No. 2 of the *Elegies* (compare the final ten measures of both examples). Meter signature changes throughout, including 6/8 + 2/8 (not + 2/4, as erroneously indicated in m. 11).

Recording

Hungaroton LPX 12334-A. *Bartók Plays and Talks*, Vol. II. Side 1, Band 1b
(No. 6), 1912.
The sound on this cylinder is too distorted for any meaningful analysis.

Notes

1. BBES, p. 433.
2. Ibid., p. 432.
3. Ibid., p. 433.
4. Hungaroton 11335, Vol. III, p. 7.
5. Complete text in the original language appears in SODO; also in BBRO, Vol. II, along with an English translation.
6. BBLE, p. 203.

Four Dirges

Op. 9a, Sz. 45
1909-1910
T6-9 M10
9' 40"

Publication

Available separately:

B&H (erroneously classified as Op. 8b)

EMB, as *Négy sirató ének*

K-BM, as *Four Nénies* (erroneously classified as Op. 8)

Included in:

EMB, publ., *Bartók Béla. Album*, Vol. II (No. 3); Vol. III (Nos. 1, 2, and 4). BBPI, Series II.

No. 2 transcribed by Bartók for orchestra (No. 3 of *Hungarian Sketches*, Sz. 97, 1931, EMB).

Commentary

In the *Four Dirges* we find some of the most vivid examples of the Debussy influence in Bartók's piano writing. Pianistic devices such as widely spaced chord formations of different registers, accumulated sonorities with the damper pedal, fragmented use of thematic material, and an atmospheric, almost hypnotic aesthetic show a strong stylistic kinship to the French Impressionist composer (it is interesting to note that the composition of the *Dirges* actually predates that of the two volumes of the Debussy *Préludes*, written in 1911-1912). László Somfai suggests that "the gradually widening and shrinking intervals of the circling melodies [found in each of the four pieces] are almost visually evocative of the movements of the mourner."[1] Each piece in the present example is a fine study in tonal balance, pedaling, and blending of tonal registers.

Movements

No. 1. Adagio. (2' 10") T6 M10

Key center B. Melody in single tones and then octaves over sustained chords. Pedal indications are given for only the first eight measures, obviously serving as a model for the pedalings in the rest of the piece. Shifting meters, octave leaps in the right hand, and long-range dynamic changes are the main difficulties.

No. 2. Andante. (2' 15") T6 M10

Key center C-sharp. Melody in octaves followed by variations that gradually enrich the harmonies and texture. The main difficulty is coordinating sustained notes and chords with melodic movement. A good sense of dynamic pacing needed because of the gradual progression from p to f over 24 measures. Five-note chords played simultaneously in both hands require a fairly large stretch and recall the final measures of No. 2 of the *Elegies*, Sz. 41.

No. 3. Poco lento. (2' 20") T6 M10

Key center G-sharp. Melody in octaves over quartal accompaniment in fourths and fifths. A good study in the pedaling of overlapping sustained tones that constantly alternate between melody and accompaniment. Since the sostenuto pedal is of little help in this instance, well-controlled and quick changes of the damper pedal (sometimes referred to as half-pedaling) are recommended. Despite the inevitable blurs that will result, the main focus should be on maintaining a consistently sustained legato in all voices.

No. 4. Assai andante. (2' 55") T9 M10

Key center G. Octave melody enveloped in widely spaced chordal textures. This is the most difficult technically of the set, mainly because of the execution and timing of the rolled chords, which can extend to as many as five octaves. The rolls should create the most unified harmonic effects possible, with the lowest chord tones included in the pedal and all rolls begun before the beat.

Note

1. Hungaroton 11335, Vol. III, p. 8.

Two Pictures (Deux Images)

Op. 12, Sz. 46
1910
T13–14 M11–14
16'

Publication

Available separately:
B&H, as *Two Images*
EMB, as *Két Kép*
K-BM
Included in:
BBPI, Series II.

Transcribed by Bartók from the original orchestral setting of the same name (also Sz. 46, 1910). Transcribed by Zoltán Kocsis for two pianos (EMB).

Commentary

Similar to the Debussy *Images* of 1905, this diptych "could be considered as a kind of homage, in acknowledgment of [Bartók's] musical debt to the French composer . . . a kind of farewell to Debussy's style as a primary shaping force in Bartók's oeuvre."[1] The editions for piano provide parenthetical instrumental indications throughout, which can be helpful in expanding the pianist's perception of instrumental sonority adapted to the piano.

Movements

No. 1. In Full Flower. Poco Adagio. (8') T13 M14
Key center D. Ternary form. The analysis of this movement by György Kroó makes reference to folk song and certain programmatic instances in *The Wooden Prince*, Sz. 60, composed five years later.[2] Because of the thick orchestration, it is not always easy to consolidate the dense texture of this piece into a solo piano setting; there are frequent instances of trills combined with scalar passages and rolled chords spanning several octaves. Although Impressionist in style, the writing does not especially lend itself to the special kind of pianistic idiom associated with Debussy and Ravel, or even with certain of Bartók's piano works of similar genre. Perhaps the two-piano arrangement by Kocsis would provide a more effective performance.

No. 2. Village (Country) Dance. Allegro. (9') T14 M11
Key center G. Rondo form (ABACA). According to Kroó, "anyone familiar with the *Two Rumanian Dances* [Sz. 43] may recognize that it was indirectly inspired by Rumanian folk music."[3] More rhythmically incisive and thinner textured than No. 1, featuring octaves and counterpoint rather than densely arrayed chordal formations. Demands keen sense of mobility, a good octave and chord-rebound technique, and the flexibility to adjust to frequent tempo changes. Al-

though technically difficult, this movement appears more pianistic than its predecessor.

Notes

1. BBPI, p. xxii.   3. Ibid.
2. KROO, p. 58.

Three Burlesques

Op. 8c, Sz. 47
No. 1, 1908; No. 2, 1911; No. 3, 1910
T9–12 M9–12
7'

Publication

Available separately:
B&H
K-BM
EMB, as *Három burlesque*

Included in:
Balógh, ed. *Bartók. Selected Works for the Piano* (Schirmer).
BBPI, Series II.

No. 2 transcribed by Bartók for orchestra (No. 4 of *Hungarian Sketches*, Sz. 97, 1931, EMB).

Commentary

Bartók's keen sense of humor is found in many instances throughout his music but is never more evident than in *Three Burlesques*. As in many piano pieces of this period, such as *Bagatelles*, Op. 6, Sz. 38, or *Suite*, Op. 14, Sz. 62, the art of musical pantomime is much in evidence, rivaling the best of Stravinsky and Prokofieff. Each piece of the set presents a highly idiomatic technical figuration, developed in patterns and registers, similar in style to that of an etude.

The set is very effective in recital as a self-contained cycle, or the pieces can be played individually, even as encores.

Movements

No. 1. Quarrel ("Discussion" in B&H). Presto. (2') T12 M9

Key center C. ABA form, with the A sections presenting octave configurations divided between the hands and B providing lyrical relief. Dedicated to Bartók's first wife, Márta Ziegler. According to László Somfai, the piece is characterized by "the confrontation of two opposing characters, full of grimaces and teasing, all this happening within a very disciplined, carefully conceived and unprogrammatic scherzo [form]."[1] Note the thematic transformation between the first subject and the "waltz" of the middle section. Suchoff cites some amusing descriptive titles and characterizations found in Bartók's first draft.[2] The opening MM marking of dotted quarter note = 96–104, found in all available editions, seems much too sluggish for the tempo indication; the dotted half must have been the intended note value. Scurrilous technical figures, whole-tone scales and chords, whimsical changes of mood, double grace notes, and downward arpeggio figures provide the main technical features. Requires imagination and wit similar to that exhibited in Schumann's "Pantelon et Columbine" (*Carnaval*, Op. 9).

No. 2. A Bit Tipsy. Allegretto. (2' 30") T9 M12

Key center E. Parallel triads prefaced by grace-note chords. Obviously a favorite of Bartók, who programmed it frequently in his recitals. Much tempo flexibility needed throughout to convey the faltering steps and meandering thoughts of the inebriate. The indication "dülöngélö ritmusban" in m. 1 (B&H) translates as "molto rubato"; "kicsit durván" in m. 16 means to play roughly or harshly; "száraz tónussal" in m. 30 is the same as "secco." In the final measures, the direction of chordal arpeggiation is indicated by arrows in some editions; in others, the symbol for the downward arpeggio is to the right of the chord.

No. 3. Capriccioso. Molto vivo, capriccioso. (2' 30") T12 M9

Key center E-flat. Freely composed, with melody mostly accompanied by swift scalar and cartwheel figurations. Much of the technical difficulty lies in the awkwardness created by frequently overlapping hands, simultaneous held and staccato notes in the same hand, and quick chordal and octave leaps. In m. 22, the lower note of the octave should read E-flat. Lightness and mobility are called for throughout, even in the climactic fortes near the end. A quick and decisive drop motion should be used to effect the accents at the tops of the cartwheel figurations (beginning in m. 58).

Recordings

Hungaroton LPX 12326-A. *Bartók at the Piano*, Vol. I. Side 1, Band 3b (No. 2), 1981/1929.
Bartók BRS 003 (No. 2), 1949/1929.
His Master's Voice AM 2622 (No. 2).

As might be expected from the characterization of No. 2, not one measure is played in strict tempo. In fact, abrupt and gradual changes in tempo, rubato effects, and agogic accents are carried far beyond, and sometimes even in opposition to, Bartók's written indications in the score. The following specific instances may be noted: "accelerando" at mm. 2, 4, 6, 8, and 10; "poco a poco accelerando" from m. 30; "rubato" (in contradiction to his "non rubato" indication, at m. 38); "vivo" at m. 42; "ritenuto" at m. 52 (where "non rubato" is also indicated). Surely these deviations from the printed page were not careless oversights on the part of Bartók, but perhaps his way of portraying the unpredictable behavior of one not in total control of his faculties.

Notes

1. Hungaroton 11336, Vol. VI, p. 7.   2. BBPI, Series II, p. xxi.

Allegro Barbaro

Sz. 49
1911
T12 M8
2' 30"

Publication

Available separately:
B&H
UE

Transcribed by Jenő Kenessey for orchestra (1946).

Commentary

One of the few single-movement works for piano, *Allegro Barbaro* represents a milestone in Bartók's compositional career. Here the composer established a truly individual style, devoid of the influences of Romanticism and Impressionism that had previously taken hold in his creative efforts. One senses a forecast of the primeval forces of his 1926 piano works, in which the martellato technique of piano writing would be used, exploiting fully the percussive properties of the instrument. Bartók himself often played this brilliant piece at the end of a piano recital or as an encore after a performance of one of his concertos. It is one of the most popular and widely played of his piano works, but also one of the most abused—by excessively impetuous interpretations.

Movement

Tempo giusto.

Key center F-sharp; combination of Phrygian, Dorian, Lydian, and non-diatonic modes. The three themes (beginning in mm. 4, 34, and 58) are subject to free development, fragmentation, and transformation of mood. Difficulties include wide octave and chordal leaps, balancing octave melodies over offbeat accompaniments, and endurance. But the main task of the performer is to avoid making the piece an avalanche of relentless noise. Stevens remarks that, were it not for Bartók's compositional checks and balances, the piece "might have degenerated into a machine-like percussion."[1] One must pay close attention to the varied dynamic range (*fff–pppp*, with just about everything in between) and the frequent instances of dynamic relief (chordal interspersions between melodic portions and the capricious middle section beginning at m. 101). Vigilant adherence to these details will help put emphasis more on the "Allegro" and less on the "Barbaro" features.

Recordings

Hungaroton LPX 12326-33. *Bartók at the Piano*, Vol. I. Side 1, Band 4, 1981/1929.

Bartók BRS 003, 1949/1929.

Hungaroton LPX 12334-38. *Bartók Plays and Talks*, Vol. II. Side 1, Band 9, 1981/1929.

Both recordings emphasize the accented melody, with the repeated-chord accompaniment very subdued. A considerably faster tempo than the prescribed MM marking of half note = 76–84 is taken (probably c. 96). Bartók takes a slight ritard at m. 33. Accented tones take on an agogic stress from m. 76.

The "poco sostenuto" at mm. 101–102 is kept at an absolute minimum to allow the right degree of forward motion to the "a tempo." One notices throughout an unmistakable melodic thread and strict attention to the indicated dynamics.

Note

1. STEV, p. 120.

Piano Method

Sz. 52
1913

Publication

Available separately:
EMB, as *Zongoraiskola*
B&H (English edition revised and edited by Leslie Russel)
Eighteen original pieces from the *Piano Method* were selected by Bartók and published separately under the title *The First Term at the Piano*, Sz. 53. See that entry for additional publication information.

Included in:
Palmer, ed. *Bartók. The First Book for Young Pianists* (Alfred).
Palmer, ed. *Bartók. An Introduction to his Piano Works* (Alfred).

The Palmer editions include introductory instructions extracted from the *Piano Method*, mainly concerning the proper execution of touch schemes for slurs, staccato, portato, tenuto, accents, and dynamics.

Commentary

Sándor Reschofsky, a specialist in elementary piano instruction, and Bartók were colleagues at the Budapest Academy of Music. They originally intended to write an instructional method that would include all phases of piano study and repertoire. According to Suchoff, five volumes were produced, the third being Bartók's edition of thirteen piano pieces from *The Little Notebook for Anna*

Magdalena Bach, his only other contribution to the project.[1] In Vol. I of the intended series, the present example, Reschofsky assumed the task of writing the basic instructional material and exercises, while Bartók composed the supplementary pieces, which were designed "to correspond exactly with the technical difficulties of the corresponding exercises." The last few pieces, etudes by Czerny and Duvernoy and a waltz by Lemoine, were intended to "include all the technical difficulties dealt with in the previous exercises."[2]

The opening material is primarily concerned with elementary theory, ear training, pitch recognition, rhythm, and conducting exercises, all of this occurring before any reference is made to the keyboard; this approach trains students in all aspects of musicianship at the very outset of their study. Technical material includes photographs of basic hand position and posture, held-note exercises, wrist exercises, thumb-crossing exercises, and a complete digest of such touch schemes as staccato, legato, portato, accents, and phrasing. Scales are introduced somewhat late in the volume, apparently to allow enough time for the more fundamental material directed toward stationary hand formations.

The *Piano Method* contains 125 examples of technical exercises interspersed with teaching pieces; the latter progress in difficulty approximately to the equivalent of Vol. III of *Mikrokosmos*, Sz. 107.

Notes

1. BBPI, Series II, xxiii.
2. Prefatory remarks to the *Piano Method* by Bartók and Reschofsky, Budapest, May 1913.

The First Term at the Piano

Sz. 52, 53
1913, 1929
T1–4 M1–5
9' 35"

Publication

Available separately:
B&H

EMB, as *Kezdők Zongoramuzsikája*
K-BM
Schott, as *Die Erste Zeit am Klavier*

Included in:

Agay, ed. *Bartók Is Easy!* (Presser).

Agay, ed. *Béla Bartók. Little Pieces and Studies* (Presser).

Alfred, publ., *Bartók. Twenty-four of his Easiest Piano Pieces.*

Alfred, publ., *Bartók. Twenty-four of his Most Popular Piano Pieces.*

Bartók-Reschofsky. *Piano Method*, Sz. 52 (B&H, EMB).

Bradley, publ., *Béla Bartók. Piano Pieces in Their Original Form.*

Brimhall, ed. *My Favorite Bartók* (Hansen).

EMB, publ., *Béla Bartók. Young People at the Piano.*

Nevin, ed. *Bartók for the Young Pianist* (Pro Art).

Novik, ed. *Young Pianist's Guide to Bartók* (Studio P/R).

Palmer, ed. *Bartók. The First Book for Young Pianists* (Alfred).

Palmer, ed. *Béla Bartók. Selected Children's Pieces for the Piano* (Alfred).

BBPI, Series II.

Commentary

The eighteen pieces in *The First Term at the Piano* were extracted from the Bartók-Reschofsky *Piano Method*, Sz. 52, and published as a separate opus in 1929. The set could well be called a *Mikrokosmos* in miniature, progressing in order of difficulty, introducing new concepts and challenges along the way, and offering a variety of styles and techniques. The level of difficulty hardly surpasses Vol. III of *Mikrokosmos*, Sz. 107, and its contents are generally more consonant and immediately appealing. It could be offered as introductory material to the later work, in which pieces of similar nature could be paired according to the following arrangement:

Sz. 53	Sz. 107
No. 1	No. 11
3	22
5	38
6	40
7	45
8	50
9	59
10	74
11	73
12	72
14	80

The MM markings in this set seem to be unreasonably slow for the appropriate musical result. But Bartók prescribed similar markings in Vol. I of *Mikrokosmos*, written more than twenty years later, so we can conclude that he had definite pedagogical objectives for these slow tempos.

Movements

The folk texts are excerpted and paraphrased from the English translations in BBHU and BBPI (Series II); complete texts in the original language appear in BBPI (Series II) and SODO.

No. 1. Moderato (No. 21 in Sz. 52). (30") T1 M1
Key center C. Two voices in parallel motion two octaves apart. Five-finger position (it should be noted that Nos. 1–10 are all in a stationary five-finger position without transposition). Four phrases of equal length. Legato touch throughout.

No. 2. Moderato (No. 22 in Sz. 52). (40") T2 M1
Key center G. Two voices in counterpoint. Seven phrases of irregular length. Legato touch throughout.

No. 3. Dialogue (No. 24 in Sz. 52). Moderato. (30") T2 M1
Key center A (right hand on tonic, left hand on dominant). Two voices in counterpoint. Irregular and overlapping phrasing. Coordination of non-coincidental rests and phrase beginnings.

No. 4. Dialogue (No. 26 in Sz. 52). Moderato. (40") T2 M1
Key center C; right hand on tonic, left hand in tetrachord position on dominant. Two voices in counterpoint. Study in irregular phrasings and non-coincidental marcatissimo accents.

No. 5. Moderato (No. 36 in Sz. 52). (35") T2 M1
Key center G. Two voices in parallel and then contrapuntal motion. Study in coincidental and non-coincidental slur-staccato combinations. Dynamic *f* unchanged throughout.

No. 6. Moderato (No. 40 in Sz. 52). (35") T2 M2
Key center A. Melody over drone-type accompaniment followed by mirrored counterpoint. Dynamic *p* unchanged throughout.

No. 7. Folk Song (No. 44 in Sz. 52). Moderato. (20") T2 M2
Key center F. Melody with variety of slur-staccato combinations over broken-chord and contrapuntal accompaniment. Contrasting dynamics introduced for the first time in the set.

No. 8. Andante (No. 51 in Sz. 52). (35") T3 M2

Key center G. Two voices in counterpoint. Crescendos *p* to *f* with *sf* accents. "Decresc." at end.

No. 9. Andante (No. 59 in Sz. 52). (35") T3 M2

Key center G; right hand on tonic, left hand in tetrachord position on dominant. Two voices in counterpoint. Alternating dynamic levels, *p* in one hand, *f* in the other. A good study in dynamic balance between the hands.

No. 10. Hungarian Folk Song (No. 68 in Sz. 52). Allegro. (30") T3 M2

> Erzsi Virág made her bed, Váczi Gábor left his hat upon it; Erzsi, bring my hat, that no maiden can look into my shining eyes [Mixed Style melody; a more poetic translation of the same text is given in Sz. 107, No. 74b].

Key center F. Melody over broken-chord accompaniment. A good technical study for the left hand. Different phrase lengths between the hands at the second repeated section.

No. 11. Minuet (No. 89 in Sz. 52). Andante. (35") T3 M3

Key center C. The first piece in the set to depart from a strict five-finger position. A study in staccato parallel sixths in both hands and coordination of touches as well as dynamics. Introduction of expression markings "grazioso" and "poco marcato." Similar to examples by Haydn and Mozart.

No. 12. Swineherd's Dance (No. 77 in Sz. 52). (50") T3 M2

Key center G; Aeolian mode. Four voices, the outer ones in tied whole notes, the inner ones with differing slur-staccato combinations, parts exchanged. Five-finger positions transposed. Echo effects at repeats. Coordination problems of held against moving voices in the same hand.

No. 13. Hungarian Folk Song (No. 95 in Sz. 52). Andante. (30") T3 M3

> Where have you been, my lambkin? [Transylvanian folk song.]

Key center G. Melody with double-note and contrapuntal accompaniment. Five-finger position abandoned in this and the rest of the pieces in the set. Slurs of varying lengths.

No. 14. Andante (No. 105 in Sz. 52). (40") T3 M3

Key center F. Two voices in free counterpoint. Syncopations at beginning reminiscent of No. 6 of the Bach *Two-Part Inventions*. Transposed from G in Sz. 52. Syncopated phrasing, increased rhythmic activity toward the end.

No. 15. Wedding Song (No. 116 in Sz. 52). Moderato. (25") T3 M3

> The cart rattles, Jancsi cracks his whip; alas, dear mother, soon they'll carry me away [song of a bride about to leave her family; Mixed Style melody].

Key center G; Dorian mode. Melody under syncopated chord accompaniment, parts exchanged. Harmonically, one of the most ingratiating of the set, with several modal implications. A study in heavy "pesante" touches involving staccato and tenuto.

No. 16. Peasant's Dance (No. 115 in Sz. 52). Allegro moderato. (15") T3 M3

Key center G; Mixolydian and Ionian modes. Melody over slur-type accompaniment. Main difficulty is control of offbeat phrasing in the right hand, each measure beginning with staccato or accent.

No. 17. Allegro deciso (No. 118 in Sz. 52). (20") T4 M3

Key center D. Four voices in expanding intervals and parallel sixths. Staccato and tenuto touches. Awkward technical situations for the fourth and fifth fingers. Syncopations requiring a good rhythmic sense.

No. 18. Waltz (No. 119 in Sz. 52). Tempo di valse. (30") T4 M5

Key center B. Melody over slur-staccato accompaniment, parts exchanged with portato touches in the right hand. A good example of simple modulation (B to E minor). A good alternative to some of the simpler Chopin waltzes.

Sonatina

Sz. 55
1915
T5–10 M4–9
3' 45"

Publication

Available separately:
Alfred (Hinson, ed.)
B&H
EMB
International (Philipp, ed.)
K-BM
Schott

Included in:
Alfred, publ., *Bartók. 24 of his Most Popular Piano Pieces.*
Balógh, ed. *Bartók. Selected Works for the Piano* (Schirmer).

K-BM, publ., *Bartók. An Album for Piano Solo*.
BBPI, Series II.

Transcribed by Bartók for orchestra (*Transylvanian Dances*, Sz. 96, 1931); by G.
Balassa for clarinet and piano; and by A. Gertler for violin and piano.

Commentary

The *Sonatina* represents the first piano cycle by Bartók to make use of authentic, as opposed to freely composed, Romanian folk material (see Sz. 43). It
makes use of five examples of instrumental peasant dances that he collected in
the Transylvanian sector of Romania from 1910 to 1914. It is also one of the
first instances in which the composer has adapted folk material for use as self-
contained concert material. Contrary to what one would expect from the title,
the movements are not cast in a modified sonata form but in freely organized
binary and ternary designs, the structures determined by the appearances of the
folk tunes. The material is presented almost unchanged from its original models
and developed by means of extensions and episodes. The set is excellent recital
material and should be performed in its entirety.

Movements

No. 1. Bagpipers. Allegretto; Allegro (32") T9 M5
Key center D; Mixolydian mode. Ternary form. According to Bartók in a
1945 radio interview, there are two themes representing "dances played by two
bagpipe players, the first by one and the second by another."[1] The pedal markings in the A section (Bartók's own) should be followed closely to convey the
continuous sound of the drone. The first of the 32d-note figures beginning at
m. 9 must be played precisely on the second beat, not before. The B section
offers difficulties in offbeat chords and control of tempo. Rhythmic precision
is required throughout.

No. 2. Bear Dance. Moderato. (32") T5 M4
Key center A; Dorian mode. Binary form with melody and accompaniment
reversed in second section. Originally played on a violin's lower strings to make
it "more similar to a bear's voice."[2] Difficulties include coordinating different
kinds of accents, especially the offbeats in the left hand, and balance of left over
right hand in the B section. The effect should be "pesante" as indicated, but
not excessively percussive.

No. 3. Finale. Allegro vivace. (1' 45") T10 M9
Key center D; Lydian (A section) and Mixolydian (B section) modes; strong
indication throughout of G tonality in the melody. Contains "two folk melodies
played by [unaccompanied] peasant violin players"[3] danced during the Christ-

mas season by a man wearing an animal costume with a moveable beak.[4] Binary form with coda combining the materials of both sections. A wide variety of dynamic, accent, articulation, and tempo indications. Difficulties include balance (m. 53, left hand, and m. 75, right hand), trill-like figurations in the B section, and timing of frequent long-range tempo and dynamic changes throughout.

Recordings

Hungaroton LPX 12329-B. *Bartók at the Piano*, Vol. I, 1981/1920. Side 8, Band 3.

Welte Legacy of Piano Treasures, No. 676, c. 1964/1920.

Although originally recorded in 1920, these discs have remarkable clarity and no distortion of sound, primarily because they were taken from piano rolls as recently as 1964. The most striking feature of No. 1 is the extreme rhythmic flexibility manifested in agogic accents (beginning in mm. 1 and 5) and the consistent acceleration to other accented tones (beginning in m. 6). These irregularities are not to be considered mannerisms but an attempt to portray the peculiarities of the Romanian bagpipe sound as Bartók himself had probably heard it. Special mention should be made of the unusually long fermata before the B section (m. 20) and the emphasis on the upbeat E at m. 49. The tempo in No. 2 is considerably faster than Bartók's indicated quarter note = 80 (more like 92–96) and seems to negate the ungainly character that one associates with the bear dance. The written-out trill figurations in the B section of No. 3 are quite prominently articulated and give the section a busy quality. As can be expected, the playing is vigorous and incisive.

Notes

1. Hungaroton LPX 12338-B, Vol. II, Side 10, Band 5.
2. Ibid.
3. Ibid.
4. BBPI, Series II, p. xxiv.

Romanian Folk Dances

Sz. 56
1915
T5–10 M4–7
4' 15"

Publication

Available separately:
B&H (No. 6 also published separately)
UE, as *Rumänische Volkstänze*
Transcribed by Bartók for orchestra (Sz. 68, 1917, UE); by L. Silva for cello
and piano; by Z. Székely for violin and piano (1926, UE); by A. Wilke for
small orchestra; and by A. Willner for string orchestra (1929, UE).

Commentary

The original title, *Romanian Folk Dances from Hungary*, was shortened by Bartók
to its present form after the Treaty of Trianon annexed Transylvania, up to
then a Hungarian territory, to Romania in 1920. The composer dedicated the
work to his Romanian friend in Belényes, Ion Busitia, who from 1909 had
prepared Bartók's collecting tours in the region. It is based on seven melodies
representing six different dance forms from four different regions in Transylvania: Bihar, Torda-Aranyos, Maros-Torda, and Torontál. The melodies were
originally played on the violin or the shepherd's flute. They are transcribed for
the piano almost unaltered but with a wide range of harmonic freedom and
novel pianistic effects. Although the work is probably performed as frequently
in its many transcriptions as in its solo piano version, it is nonetheless a welcome addition to any piano recital and is most effective if played in its entirety.

Movements

No. 1. Joc cu Bâtă (Dance with Sticks). Allegro moderato. (55") T7 M4
Key center A; Dorian and Aeolian modes. Melody with bass-chord accompaniment. Played on two violins, one playing the melody, the other (a three-
stringed instrument) playing chords on the strong beats. According to Bartók,
it is a "young men's solo dance, with various figures the last of which—as a
consummation—consists of kicking the room's ceiling!"[1] A good study in left-
hand leaps and a wide variety of slurs, accents, and staccatos occurring simultaneously between the hands. If the pedal is used exactly as indicated in the
editions listed above, many of the articulations in the top melody will be excessively blurred; in fact, much of the piece can be played effectively with no pedal
at all. In Bartók's notated version of the original folk setting, mm. 45–46 are
marked "pizz.," suggesting a crisp finger staccato (mm. 29–30 of the piano version).

No. 2. Brâul (Waistband Dance). Allegro. (25") T5 M7
Key center D; Dorian mode. Melody (originally a flute solo) with bass-chord

accompaniment. "This dance is performed at gatherings in the spinning house, generally only by girls, sometimes by young men and girls. They hold each other, their arms tightly clasped around each other's [waists], and form a circle. . . ."[2] A delicate, graceful miniature, requiring a good sense of rubato and poetic phrasing. As in No. 1, the pedal indications are excessive and can easily be avoided. The repeat can be played *pp*.

No. 3. Pe Loc (On the Spot). Andante. (45") T6 M6

Key center B; melody (originally a flute solo) with augmented second suggesting Arabic influence, which is occasionally found in Romanian folk music. The narrow range of the melody and accompaniment is in keeping with the nature of the original folk setting, in which the dancers do not move from their location. In this instance, the pedal indications seem correct, their length enhancing the continuous sound of the drone in the left hand while not blurring the high-register melody. The ornamented tones (beginning in m. 5) are to be played as triplets, on the beat, with a light accent on the first note. Delicacy of touch required in the right hand.

No. 4. Buciumeana (Butschum [Transylvania]). Moderato. (35") T8 M7

Key center A; Mixolydian and Arabic modes. Melody (originally a violin solo) with bass-chord accompaniment in hemiola rhythm. This example is cited by Bartók as the first of the three categories of transcribed folk music, in which "the used folk melody is the more important part of the work. The added accompaniment and eventual preludes and postludes may only be considered as the mounting of a jewel."[3] The main difficulty is in the left hand, where wide stretches and multiple voicings require precise fingerings. The pedal indications are recommended to facilitate the legato in the left hand. The melody should be played with particular attention to legato and precise slurring.

No. 5. Poargă Românească (Romanian Polka). Allegro. (30") T9 M4

Key center D; Lydian mode. Melody with bass-chord accompaniment. Alternating meters of 2/4 and 3/4, although the original notation is in a consistent 2/4. A children's dance of a crisp and lively nature, requiring finger strength and punctuated staccatos. The grace-note/main-note combinations (which are two sixteenth notes in the original notation) are best played with one stroke, almost simultaneously. Pedal indications would seem to need modification. Cross-hand coordination problems and some awkward reaches in the left hand.

No. 6. Mărunțel (Fast Dance). Allegro; Più allegro. (35") T10 M6

Key center A; hint of D Lydian at the opening. (Originally a violin solo.) Two melodies with syncopated chordal accompaniment for each. "Dance (en deux), performed by many couples," similar to a courting dance.[4] Requires stamina and the ability to coordinate the many rhythmic syncopations that occur. The MM marking at the "Più allegro" is only slightly faster than that of the opening melody (quarter note = 144 vs. 132) and should not be rushed. The alternative ("Ossia") notation does not significantly enhance the musical effect. Pay particular attention to the right-hand fingering patterns beginning in m. 56. A brilliantly effective ending to the set.

Recordings

Hungaroton LPX 12328-B. *Bartók at the Piano*, Vol. I, 1981/1930. Side 6, Band 5 (Székely, violin; Bartók, piano).

Columbia M6X 31513, 1972/1930.

Hungaroton LPX 12329-B. *Bartók at the Piano*, Vol. I, 1981/1920. Side 8, Band 4.

Welte Legacy of Piano Treasures, No. 676, c. 1964/1920.

Hungaroton LPX 12334-A. *Bartók Plays and Talks*, Vol. II. Side 1, Band 4 and 5, c. 1915.

The 1930 recording is of the 1926 arrangement by Zoltán Székely for violin and piano. As can be expected, the piano accompaniment offers some interesting alterations, both texturally and harmonically, from the solo piano version. The 1920 recording, this time for solo piano, also incorporates a certain degree of interpretive license in the form of added ornamentation and varied repeats. The performance is free-spirited with much rhythmic flexibility. In Nos. 1 and 2, we find a generous but discreet use of pedal, in keeping with the indications in the score, although one is hardly aware of any blurs. In No. 1, Bartók ornaments the C at m. 21 with a *Schleifer* (slide), suggesting a performance practice normally associated with the Baroque. In the repetition of No. 2, he adds octave doubling to the melody; No. 4 is similiarly treated, even though the score lacks the repeat sign, and altered harmonically. Both Nos. 5 and 6 are played at least 20 degrees faster than Bartók's prescribed MM indication of quarter note = 132 but are under such control that they never seem inappropriately fast.

Notes

1. BBRO, Vol. I, p. 40.
2. Ibid., p. 39.
3. BBES, p. 351.
4. BBRO, Vol. I, p. 40.

Romanian Christmas Songs

Sz. 57
1915

Publication

Available separately:
B&H
UE, as *Rumänische Weihnachtslieder*
Transcribed by P. Arma for mixed choir (*Hirtenlieder zur Weihnachtszeit*).
Although these pieces were originally written to avoid stretches of an octave
or more, Bartók later provided enlargements to some of them, mainly in the
form of octave doublings, to make them more suitable for concert performance;
they are included as an appendix in UE. The following pieces are subject to
these alterations: Series I, Nos. 3, 5, 6, and 8; Series II, Nos. 2, 4, 5, 7, 8, 9,
and 10.

Commentary

This two-volume set, ten pieces in each, is based on melodies Bartók collected from 1909 in the Transylvanian sector of Romania (then a territory of
Hungary). These songs, or *Colinde*, were customarily sung on Christmas Eve
by young men and women, who would go from house to house in their villages
and receive gifts. The texts, as might be expected, are based on liturgical themes
about the birth of Christ, but many of them have alternative texts that are purely pagan in origin. The liturgical texts are usually interspersed with refrains of
a laudatory nature, explaining to some extent the melodic and rhythmic
peculiarities of the songs. Each volume is designed to be played as a continuous
unit, each piece leading directly into the next. Unlike the metrically consistent
tempo giusto of the Romanian dance sections in Sz. 55 and 56, meters in this example are quite irregular, sometimes changing every measure, suggesting
similarities to Bulgarian folk music. This collection is probably the least known
of the Romanian piano settings of 1915, quite possibly because it had been out
of print for some time. However, a performance of perhaps one of the volumes
with the elaborations in UE could be a perfectly acceptable recital group and
could introduce some of the more lyrical and refined examples of Bartók's piano
writing.

Movements

The folk texts in Series I and II are excerpted and paraphrased from the English translations in BBRO, Vol. IV, and personally acquired sources; complete texts in the original language appear in BBRO (Vol. IV), SODO, and the B&H and UE editions.

Series I
T3–8 M3–6
4′ 45″

No. 1. Allegro. (35″) T5 M4

> Through that mountain meadow, sheep are going. But who is walking ahead of them? Lo the shepherd. . . . [Refrain:] Lord God, hoy, to the Almighty!

Key center E; Dorian mode. Three variations with drone accompaniment and occasional counterpoint. Coordination problems of held against moving voices of different touches in the same hand. Frequent alternation of duple and triple meters.

No. 2. Allegro. (20″) T4 M4

> They are asking the saints of the Lord, "of what is made the wine, the wheat, and the holy oil? . . ." [Refrain:] To the almighty, to the dear Lord!

Key center G; Ionian mode. Two variations, melody in different registers with chordal accompaniment. Meter alternates between 5/8, 2/4, and 3/8. Interlocking hands.

No. 3. Allegro. (40″) T6 M4

> The youthful bridegroom is praying. . . . [Refrain:] To the Lord Almighty!

Key center D; Aeolian mode. Three variations with varied accompaniment patterns. Meter signature at the beginning of the piece (4/8, 3/8) indicates alternating measures. A good study in the tenuto touch.

No. 4. Andante. (35″) T4 M5

> Let us come inside; the rain is pouring and our horses have gone lame, and they should be shod with horseshoes of pastry and with nails of sausage. [Refrain:] For the Almighty!

Key center D; Dorian mode (melody suggests A Phrygian). Two variations, melody in different registers with chordal and linear accompaniment. A variety of touches in right-hand melody. Syncopations in the left hand (beginning in m. 16) could cause some difficulty.

No. 5. Allegro moderato. (25″) T6 M4

Come to me, come to me, beloved Ileana!

Key center G; Aeolian mode. Three variations with accompaniment in parallel intervals. Perhaps the opening *f* dynamic should be modified somewhat to avoid harshness in the "più f" statement.

No. 6. Andante. (35") T3 M5

In all the world's four corners all who bear the name of mankind shall be called to go to judgment. . . . [Refrain:] Yearning may cast me down!

Key center E; Phrygian and Aeolian modes. Two variations, each in different voices with linear accompaniment. Good study in legato and coordinating held against moving voices in the same hand.

No. 7. Andante. (25") T4 M6

At a quiet well-spring, [Refrain:] To the Lord Almighty!

Key center E; Dorian mode. Three variations with swaying left-hand accompaniment supplementing the rhythm of the melody and becoming increasingly more active harmonically. Meter signature at beginning (2/8, 3/8, 3/8) indicates the pulses within the measure rather than alternating measures, as in No. 3 (compare the same treatment in "Six Dances in Bulgarian Rhythm," Vol. VI of *Mikrokosmos*, Sz. 107). Exact differentiation needed of the grace-note slurs (played as 32d notes) and the sixteenth-note slurs. Note how the accompaniment figure is transformed in the final five measures to forecast that of No. 8.

No. 8. Allegretto. (40") T8 M5

Upon the foot bridge, flocks of stalwarts cross leading finely harnessed horses. An old woman asks of them, "Have you seen the Holy Son?" . . . [Refrain:] Oh Lord Almighty!

Key center G; Dorian mode. Five variations, melody in different voices with alternating octave accompaniment. The most difficult piece in Series I. Parallel first-inversion triads played in quick succession result in tricky fingering. Mixed meter signature of 2/4 and 3/4 indicates alternating measures.

No. 9. Allegro. (15") T6 M4

Let all fellows and worthy deacons sing praises and rejoice!

Key center C; Mixolydian mode. Three variations, melody in different registers with varied accompaniment. A difficult piece to coordinate because of the offbeat accompaniment patterns and varying touches that occur simultaneously between the hands.

No. 10. Più allegro. (15") T5 M3

Three kings from the rising sun, with the star went journeying, to see and to know Him, and to Christ bring their devotion.

Key center F; Ionian mode. Variation with extension. Shifting meters. Chordal texture with richly varied harmonies. An effective ending to the series.

Series II
T4–9 M3–6
6' 5"

No. 1. Molto moderato. (45") T5 M5

There, below the mountain, there are three flocks of sheep, and of the three shepherd lads with them, only one is a stranger. . . . [Refrain:] Flowers, the white apple blossoms!

Key center G; Aeolian mode. Four variations with melody in different registers; basically contrapuntal accompaniment. Problems in maintaining a smooth legato with two voices in one hand.

No. 2. Moderato. (25") T4 M5

On the highest hill, the holy sun has arisen, which sheds light upon the world and brings the summer back again. . . . [Refrain:] For the Lord, for the Almighty!

Key center G; Ionian mode. Two variations, basically chordal textures. Lilting barcarolle style asks for a delicate touch and a supple rhythmic sense. The designation eighth = quarter note at m. 7 is merely a reminder of the change in metric unit, not a change in the duration of the notes.

No. 3. Andante. (25") T5 M5

Make them grow, Lord, rear them, all sons the world over; rear me, Lord, and my own son as well. . . . [Refrain:] Grant the Lord Almighty!

Key center B; Aeolian mode (harmonic form). Melodically, texturally, and rhythmically, this piece is strikingly similar to No. 1.

No. 4. Andante. (45") T5 M5

You great lords, wake up your daughters, so that they may set the table, sweep the mansion, and fill the glasses for the carolers and the Lord. . . . [Refrain:] Lord, let's carol!

Key center D; Dorian mode. Three variations displaying contrapuntal and chordal textures. A good study in legato and poetic phrasing.

No. 5. Moderato. (30") T7 M4

A young maiden sits on her bed and sobs, for she has lost her white necklace of old coins and her earrings; good lads, if you don't give me back what you took, I've three brothers like men. . . . [Refrain:] To the Almighty!

Key center D; Dorian mode. Three variations with the melody in different registers and varied accompaniments. A brusque piece requiring a weighty touch and rhythmic deliberation.

No. 6. Andante. (55", 25") T5 M5

Lo, a band of youthful carolers set off on the way on the long journey; the Virgin Mary appeared and asked them if they had seen the Holy Son.

Key center G; Mixolydian mode. Four variations with similar accompaniment patterns but different harmonic backgrounds. Mixed meters. The prevailing interval of the augmented second and the small melodic compass suggest Arabic style, which is sometimes found in Romanian folk music. The figurations in the bass clef require large stretches and a pliable hand. The melody is presented again with an additional two variations between Nos. 7 and 8 of this series.

No. 7. Variante della precedente [this is a misprint in B&H and UE; it belongs to the restatement of No. 6]. (20") T5 M3

At the quiet well-spring was resting the Lord God and the Virgin Mary and a small Son.

Key center D; Mixolydian mode. Three variations with the melody in different registers with an assortment of accompaniment patterns, harmonies, and articulations. In variations 1 and 2, the accompaniment figures often overlap the melodies, causing the hands to interlock.

No. 8. Allegro. (30") T4 M4

There has waxed and is risen a star beautiful and bright; even before it arose, wise men read of it in books. . . . [Refrain:] I'm caroling, Lord!

Key center F-sharp; Ionian mode with lowered sixth. Two variations, the melody in the right hand in the first and in the left in the second. Note the change in melodic articulation between variations (tenuto-staccato vs. portato).

No. 9. Allegretto. (25") T7 M4

Happiness is his, the good gentleman and old nobleman; the dear Lord has bestowed happiness upon him. . . . [Refrain:] Hoy, to the Almighty!

Key center F; Ionian mode. Three variations, each with the melody in a different register and with a different harmonic pattern. Mixed meters. Difficult offbeat accompaniment patterns and slurs.

No. 10. Allegro. (40") T9 M6

Let us all climb up to the town of Bethlehem, unto Mary let's bring gifts. . . .
[Refrain:] Hoy, sing among the apple blossoms!

Key center C; Ionian mode. Five variations with development between the
third and the fourth. Mixed meter. A witty and brilliantly effective ending to
the set. Requires quick chord-rebound facility at a soft dynamic. Note the
canon beginning in m. 13 and the non-coincident bar lines, which preserve the
irregular metric structure of the original tune.

Suite

Op. 14, Sz. 62
1916
T7–13 M9–12
7' 55"

Publication

Available separately:
B&H
UE

It has recently been discovered that the *Suite* was originally conceived with
five movements. The extra movement, an "Andante," was to be placed between Nos. 1 and 2, but it was ultimately deleted by Bartók. The "Andante"
was published in the October 1955 issue of *Új Zenei Szemle (New musical review)*
and eventually fell into the possession of one of Bartók's former pupils.[1]

Béla Siki provides a detailed commentary on the *Suite* in *Piano Repertoire. A
Guide to Interpretation and Performance* [SIKI], pp. 317-28.

Commentary

According to Bartók in a 1944 radio interview, this work represents a continuation of a new trend of piano writing, inaugurated in the *Bagatelles*, Op. 14,
Sz. 38, and continued in the *Sonata*, Sz. 80.[2] In it he sought to refine piano
technique into a simpler and more transparent style and to avoid the excesses
of his earlier post-Romantic piano writing. Although the *Suite* is the only work

produced during the period 1914–1917 that is not based on original folk melodies, there is an unmistakable similarity to folk material in some of the movements, especially of Romanian (No. 1) and Arabic (No. 3) origins. Much experimentation with whole-tone and other scale patterns, and one can even find a twelve-tone row in No. 2, probably the only instance in Bartók's entire piano writing.

Movements

No. 1. Allegretto. (1' 50") T12 M11

Key center B-flat. ABA form, section A presenting melody with offbeat accompaniment patterns, section B retaining basically the same texture while presenting contrasting material, and the return of section A fragmenting the melodic components of the opening theme. Related to Romanian folk music by virtue of its patterns of an eighth and two sixteenth notes and its regular phrase structure. Much emphasis on the whole-tone scale and tritone relationships. The greatest difficulties occur in mm. 52–76, where the hands often interlock; hands should be practiced together to determine their exact positioning at all times (e.g., keep the right hand *sopra* in mm. 70–71 and *sotto* in mm. 72–73). Lightness of touch, maintaining a melodic thread throughout, and coordination of offbeat slurs and staccato accompaniment patterns are the primary requirements of this popular piece.

No. 2. Scherzo. (1' 50") T12 M12

Key center B-flat. Rondo form (ABACABA). Ascending and descending augmented triads and chromatically shifting octaves constitute the principal theme, the episodes offering more lyrical statements. Example of twelve-tone rows, mm. 17–24. A study in the martellato type of staccato, in which reinforced fingers (1 + 2 or 2 + 3) are needed for maximum power. In addition to the bracketed pedal indications, pedal should be used in mm. 97–98 and 103–104 so that the low C's can be sustained.

No. 3. Allegro molto. (2') T13 M9

Key center D. ABA form. Left-hand ostinato figure with repeated-note melodic figures. Scale patterns of Arabic origin, a result of Bartók's collecting tours in Algeria in 1913. In section A, care should be taken that clarity is achieved in the extreme lower registers with the indicated "non troppo legato" touch. Although rhythmic vitality is essential, dynamic restraint is extremely important, especially at the very opening; note that the first *f* does not occur until m. 29 and lasts only two measures. The B section ("Poco più mosso") should not be given to extremes of percussiveness, despite the "ff martellato" indication; be sure to save strength for the sforzandos to follow and to hold the pedal tones in the left hand for full value. "However difficult the movement is, the performance will gain impressiveness through an easy, unforced virtuosity and a big, but still elegant, tone."[3]

No. 4. Sostenuto. (2' 15") T7 M12

Key center B-flat. ABA form, the return of section A serving more the function of a coda. This hauntingly beautiful piece has as its main idea a three-note motive (B, C, C-flat, the same motive that permeates No. 3) that undergoes extensive melodic development. A keen sense of tonal balance is required at the very beginning, where the main melody is encased in the chordal accompaniment, and subsequently, where subtle and delicate counterpoint takes place. "Bartók made it evident here that control over tone can be a real difficulty, severely taxing the artistry and imagination of the performer."[4] The short B section is difficult to memorize. Although one has the option of using the sostenuto pedal to connect the bass tones, half pedals might be a better way to achieve the atmospheric quality needed. Under no circumstances should Nos. 3 and 4 be interchanged in order to achieve a brilliant ending to the set!

Recordings

Hungaroton LPX 12326-A. *Bartók at the Piano*, Vol. I, 1981. Side 1, Band 5, 1929; Side 1, Band 6, 1929.
His Master's Voice AN 486, 1930.
Bartók BRS 003, c. 1949, 1929.

These recordings have been well preserved over the years and are performed with dazzling brilliance. The brisk tempos indicated in the MM markings of the fast movements are successfully maintained with generally no loss of clarity, rhythmic conviction, or control. In No. 1, the opening melody is treated with a poetic and folk-like simplicity, with explicit attention to the dynamic indications. "(Pedal)" at m. 21 is only sparingly observed to maintain the staccatos and abrupt cutoffs called for. No real loss of forward motion occurs in the more lyrical sections (beginning in m. 37), although much elasticity of phrasing is felt. A fascinating interplay of accents is heard throughout, mainly because of the strict adherence to them. Because of the fast tempos and rhythmic buoyancy, Nos. 1 and 2 are metrically perceived as having one beat per measure; the latter movement even has a gigue-like momentum that can be interpreted as some kind of compound or quadruple meter. The lyrical sections (beginning in mm. 33 and 163) are played progressively more slowly and plaintively so that the final "Tranquillo" and "Tempo I" receive the utmost in contrast. The frenetic pace of No. 3 is held in check by slight enunciations of the left-hand downbeats to counteract the many syncopations that occur. Other notable features include: a small degree of ritard before the chords at mm. 50 and 54 to facilitate the connections; an agogic stress on the accented first and third beats of mm. 80–83, giving them almost a quarter-and-eighth-note appearance; and virtually no slowing down to accommodate for the difficulties beginning in m. 113. The emphasis in No. 4 seems to be more of melodic definition and direction than subtlety and delicacy; nowhere does the momentum falter. Again, one hears the agogic accents on the first of the slurs at the "Più sostenuto" section.

Notes

1. CROW, pp. 137-138.   3. SIKI, p. 327.
2. BBES, p. 432.   4. Ibid., p. 328.

Three Hungarian Folk-Tunes

Sz. 66
1914–1917
T5–8 M7–9
3' 40"

Publication

Available separately:
B&H

Included in:
Homage to Paderewski (B&H, 1942); compositions by fifteen other prominent composers of the period are also represented in this memorial album.

No. 3 transcribed by Tibor Serly as "Preludium" to *Suite from Mikrokosmos*.

Commentary

It is likely that this set was originally intended for inclusion in *Fifteen Hungarian Peasant Songs*, Sz. 71, written around the same period. On its own, however, the work has much to offer musically in such a short time-span. It can be effectively programmed as a recital opener or as a companion set to one of Bartók's folk-dance cycles.

Movements

The folk texts are excerpted and paraphrased from the English translations in BBHU and personally acquired sources; complete texts in the original language appear in BBHU and SODO.

No. 1. Andante tranquillo, rubato. (1') T5 M9

> Down comes a peacock by the town hall; in his beak he carries water to each of the prisoners [Old Style melody; the peacock is symbolic of the oppressive ruling class].

Key center G; Mixolydian mode. Two variations with coda. Expressive octave playing is needed in the right hand. Long-range tempo and dynamic changes need careful gauging. A good study in rubato.

No. 2. Allegro non troppo, un poco rubato. (1' 15") T7 M9

> On the market-place at Jánoshida the boy-market takes place this week, and I shall go to select one. Don't buy a fair one, he'll be too weak; nor a red one, he'll be too fond of drink; but a dark one, he'll be inclined to kissing [New Style melody].

Key center A; Dorian mode. Two variations, each with extension; the end of each three-measure phrase corresponds with an exclamatory statement ("i-ca-te") acting as a refrain. Main melody divided in octaves between the hands, with offbeat chordal accompaniment; take care that these chords do not eclipse the sustained melody above. Varied echo-like repetitions of the last lines of each of the two variations. Some tricky two-voice counterpoint, sometimes overlapping, in the second variation. Shifting meters of 2/4 and 3/4.

No. 3. Maestoso. (1' 35") T8 M7

> White lily, jump into the Tesza [river]; yellow lily, jump into the Danube [Mixed Style melody].

Key center G; Mixolydian mode. Four variations with developmental coda. Some difficult slur coordinations in variations 2 and 3 and widely spaced rolled chords in variation 4. Effective coda in the style of a fanfare, a rare occurrence in Bartók's folk-song settings but a very fitting opening to Serly's transcription. Note the left-hand statement in octaves of the opening motive in m. 16.

Recordings

Hungaroton LPX 12326-33. *Bartók at the Piano*, Vol. I, 1981. Side 16, Band 4, c. 1941.

Continental CLP 101, c. 1949, c. 1941.

Turnabout/Vox THS 65010. *Bartók Plays Bartók*, 1974. Side 2, Band 3.

Rubato is very pronounced in No. 1, with accelerando at the 2/4 measures and agogic accents on the first beats of the following 3/4 measures. Nos. 2 and 3 are somewhat faster than Bartók's prescribed MM markings of quarter note = 92 and 90 respectively. The persistent quarter-note melody of No. 3 is treated with a somewhat irregular rhythmic pulse, the quarter notes being grouped as if they were two-note slurs with agogic stresses on their initial tones.

Fifteen Hungarian Peasant Songs

Sz. 71
1914–1917
T3–12 M4–11
11' 35"

Publication

Available separately:
B&H (No. 6 also published separately)
UE

Transcribed by P. Arma for flute and piano (*Paysanne Hongroise*) and for flute and string orchestra (*Paysanne Hongroise*); and by P. Mosonyi for violin and piano (Universal). Nos. 6–12, 14, and 15 transcribed by Bartók for orchestra (*Hungarian Peasant Songs*, Sz. 100, UE, B&H, 1939). Nos. 7–12 transcribed by Tibor Polgár for orchestra (*Old Hungarian Dances*, 1927).

Commentary

For the first time since Vol. I of *For Children*, Sz. 42, written in 1908–1909, we find an example of a piano cycle devoted exclusively to Hungarian folk music. Its composition points the way to some of Bartók's more advanced techniques of folk-song transcription, which are to find their apotheosis in *Improvisations*, Op. 20, Sz. 74. While the pieces in the present example follow the original tunes closely, one discovers more elaborate use of episodic material, more varied use of harmonic and pianistic effects, and more organic development and transformation of thematic material than in previous works of similar nature. All three classes of Hungarian folk music (Old Style, New Style, Mixed Style) are represented in the collection and assume equal importance with the material in the piano settings. Programming the work seems to be a matter of personal preference, some sources regarding it as a unified whole, even similar to a four-movement sonata,[1] others suggesting more latitude in choosing movements or sections to be played.[2] Although Bartók probably never performed the work in its entirety, pieces should be joined when not separated by a full double bar (e.g., Nos. 1–4 and 7–15).

Movements

The folk texts are excerpted and paraphrased from the English translations in BBHU and personally acquired sources; complete texts in the original language appear in BBHU and SODO.

Four Old Tunes

No. 1. Rubato. (45″) T6 M11

> I tie my horse to a weeping willow and bow my head toward him in grief [Old Style melody].

Key center D; Aeolian mode. Two variations, each using melody with strumming accompaniment. This and Nos. 2, 3, and 4 are examples of the Old Style, for which a grasp of the *parlando-rubato* style of execution is essential. Note the differences between the broken and continuous rolled chords. Subtle changes in nuance are indicated by the slight differences in accent markings in the repetition.

No. 2. Andante. (1′ 45″) T6 M11

> Stay, stay, you little bird, My ailing heart has long awaited you; sick I am with love, comfort the sadness of my soul [Mixed Style melody].

> The flower given by my love did not wither yet when he left me for another woman; alas, may God punish her, alas!

Key center D; Dorian mode. Two variations interspersed with introduction, interlude, and coda. Note frequent tempo changes (the "Più andante" means slightly faster), and the fragmented melody (stems pointing up) in the introduction and interlude. The left hand is awkwardly positioned in its melodic statement, second variation.

No. 3. Poco rubato. (35″) T3 M10

> Sun, O sun, shine in all thy brightness, not in mist enshrouded [Old Style melody].

> Ah! Where are you going, you three orphans? We embark on a long journey to find work as servants.

Key center F-sharp; Phrygian mode. One variation. Short but interpretively difficult. The first note of the melody (preceded by a grace-note) is an exclamatory "Aj" in the text. Pay attention to rhythmic subtleties and durations of note values. Can be repeated with octave doubling in the melody.

No. 4. Andante. (30") T7 M9

> If you did know, my angel, you loved me not, why did you not write me a farewell letter? [Old Style melody].

Key center F-sharp; Dorian mode. One variation. Mixed meters. The main difficulty lies in the interplay between octave melody and chordal interspersions, requiring quick jumps and precise pedaling to avoid blurring of the melody (in m. 1, be sure the D-sharp in the melody is released when pedaling the B).

No. 5. Scherzo. Allegro. (45") T9 M10

> My wife is so clean, she washes only once a month; all my life I'll regret getting married! [Mixed Style melody].

Key center C; Dorian mode. Four variations of diverse character. Melody in different registers. A humorous digression from "Four Old Tunes." Note the differences in melodic articulations with each variation. Grace-note figures must be light and unobtrusive (in the opening the same effect can be achieved in the right hand by rolling the figures from top to bottom, D-E-F-sharp-G). A good encore.

No. 6. Ballad. Andante. (2' 25") T8 M11

> [The story of Angoli Borbála, a tragedy of 23 verses ending in the death of two lovers—Old Style melody.]

Key center G; Dorian mode. Ten variations of diverse character. Shifting meters, changing tempos and key centers. In the first four variations, pay particular attention to the 7/8 meter and the harmonic enrichment achieved by the double stems in the left hand. Variations 6-8 (mm. 21-34) are truly rhapsodic transformations of the original material and correspond roughly to verses 15-18 of the text. Similar to the Brahms *Ballades*, Op. 10, in its adherence to a clearly defined story line. Dramatic temperament needed.

Old Dance Tunes

No. 7. Allegro. (35") T7 M5

Come, follow where I go; you will soon know where I live: By the hedge of haw-
thorn, Come, my love, unto my arms [Old Style melody].

Key center C; Dorian mode. Four variations. Needs good octave technique
and the ability to emphasize inner voices in the first variation. The septuplet
figures connecting the second and third variations should be played in a glissando manner and not rushed; note the breath mark before the final septuplet.
"(Ped.)" at m. 28 means pedal *ad libitum*. The dramatic effect of variation 4
(beginning at m. 40) will be heightened by clear enunciation of the chord changes; note the countermelody hinted at in the left-hand chords.

No. 8. Allegretto. (30") T4 M8

Climbing the plum-tree, I tore my breeches; ah well, my little girl will mend them
[Old Style melody].

Key center G; Dorian mode. Two variations. Good study in offbeat melodic
stresses and legato chord changes. Rubato effects and subtle mood changes take
place in this short piece.

No. 9. Allegretto. (10") T7 M4

You were good and sweet at night; you lay down and slept after coming home
drenched and kissing me warmly [New Style melody].

The girls spin the flax, they keep saying among themselves: "Oh, Mother, the
spinning is hard, the waiting is hard."

Key center D; Dorian mode. Four variations (2 + 2) divided by No. 10,
which acts as a trio in an ABA form. The main difficulties are the different
sets of durations and syncopations with each voice. A drone effect should be
achieved giving the tied notes their full value.

No. 10. L'istesso tempo (as in No. 9). (10") T4 M4

The grasshopper in the green forest would mate with the fly [Old Style melody].

Key center B; Dorian mode. Two variations. Lightness of touch and crisp
staccato contrast with "pesante" quality of No. 9.

No. 11. Assai moderato. (50") T6 M7

Fade away rose, you do not belong to me; if you did, you would blossom far better [Mixed Style melody].

You are no woman; you do not dare to kiss me; perhaps you think I cannot
return it [tune "mostly sung with bagpipe accompaniment"[3]].

Key center A; Dorian mode. Three variations, each of increasing intensity.
The indication "a 3 battute" means that three measures are to be grouped as

<

though they were one measure of three beats; the phrasing is to be in accordance with this grouping. The discrepancy in rolled chords is by no means arbitrary but must be followed precisely as written for the proper effect (e.g., the chords not rolled usually indicate a de-emphasis in the phrasing, occurring at the ends of the three-measure units). A bold, pompous interpretation is called for.

No. 12. Allegretto. (30") T8 M9

By the Danube there's a mill that grinds worries to shreds, hey ha! I have many worries, so I'll take them there and have them ground, hey ha! [Mixed Style melody].

Sick woman, tired lad; play a song for me you Gypsy lad, hey ha! Wait a little, while I eat my fill, then I will play a lively dance, hey ha!

Key center A; Aeolian mode with raised seventh (harmonic minor); raised third at final cadences. An example of a melodic structure in which "the second half of the melodies is approximately the repetition of the first half, lower by a fifth."[4] The cadential chords at mm. 5 and 10 and similar places in subsequent variations correspond to the exclamatory "ejeha!" statements in the text. Three variations (2 + 1) divided by No. 13, which acts as a trio in an ABA form. Difficulties include irregular slur-staccato combinations and syncopations in the same hand, left-hand octaves in the second variation, and keeping a light touch throughout.

No. 13. Poco più vivo (as compared with No. 12). (15") T7 M5

I bought my fine horse Sári only yesterday from Szolnok; nevertheless I will sell him today for wine and a beautiful woman [Old Style melody].

Key center D; Aeolian mode. One variation. Double-note slurs and offbeat chords are the main difficulties.

No. 14. Allegro. (30") T9 M5

The girls of Izsap kneaded dumplings, ho-hum, hey-ha [Mixed Style melody].

Key center C-sharp; Phrygian mode. Four variations with modulation to No. 15. The two-note slur figures at mm. 5 and 6 and in subsequent variations correspond to the exclamatory statements "M-hm, éj-ha" in the text. Basically the same technical difficulties as in No. 13 plus quick chord-rebound figures.

No. 15. Allegro. (1' 20") T12 M6

"Hungarian bagpipe music, taken unaltered from a phonograph record and provided with an accompaniment. . . ."[5]

Key center B-flat; Mixolydian, Ionian modes. *Cornemuse* is a generic term for the bagpipe. The indication "Ped. sempre" should be adhered to throughout to enhance the drone effect, with changes as the need arises. "To keep such a passage from sounding excessively blurred, the player must make certain to give the bass a firm support, paying special attention to the downbeat accents."[6] The coordination difficulties in this example are severe: left-hand offbeat slurs and broken chords, slur and held-note combinations in the right hand, and grace-note configurations in the "Più vivo." The indication "Poco più meno vivo" at m. 72 means "a little slower." Much drill, hands separately, is needed to master the technical requirements of this finale.

Recordings

Hungaroton LPX 12326. *Bartók at the Piano*, Vol. I, 1981. Side 2, Band 2
   (Nos. 7–10, 12, 14, and 15), c. 1936.
Bartók BRS 903, c. 1950/1936.
Hungaroton LPX 12329. *Bartók at the Piano*, Vol. I, 1981. Side 8, Band 1b
   (No. 6), c. 1920; Side 8, Band 2 (Nos. 7–10, 12, 14, and 15), c. 1920.
Welte Legacy of Piano Treasures, Album No. 676, c. 1964/1920.

It is curious that, despite the time lapse between the 1920 and 1936 recordings, Nos. 11 and 13 are omitted in both instances. Because the 1920 recording was taken from piano rolls as recently as 1964, the Welte version has more clarity and less distortion than the 1936 presentation. No. 6 receives a poignantly sensitive reading, each of its variations vividly portraying the turn of events in the story; it should be noted that at the "Poco adagio" the octaves are rolled in a continuous manner, from bottom to top. Despite the inherent pungency and angularity of the dance rhythms in "Old Dance Tunes," many of the accents and syncopations are subdued in favor of a more lyrical approach, especially in the 1936 version. One also hears a liberal amount of rubato and is constantly made aware of character variations with each new strophe. Also in the later recording, some of the tempos depart from the printed indications, especially in Nos. 12 (slower than indicated), 14 (faster), and 15 (much faster).

Notes

1. GRIF, p. 26.
2. KROO, p. 79.
3. BBES, p. 247.

4. Ibid., p. 306.
5. Ibid., p. 262.
6. BANO, p. 75.

Three Studies

Op. 18, Sz. 72
1918
T14-15+ M9-14
7' 15"

Publication

Available separately:
B&H

Commentary

This collection is a valuable contribution to the etude repertory of the twentieth century, although it is smaller in scope and inclusiveness than the two-volume sets of Chopin and Debussy. The present example focuses on unique and idiomatic technical problems, primarily those concerned with the expansion and contraction of the hand. The *Studies* are also significant from an analytical point of view, presenting compositional techniques that point to Bartók's more advanced musical language of the 1920s. They are extremely demanding technically and require much physical and mental endurance despite their short length. One can program them as a complete set or individually; Nos. 1 and 2 are the most likely to stand on their own in a group of miscellaneous piano works by Bartók or other etudes.

Movements

No. 1. Allegro molto. (2' 5") T15+ M9
Key center B. Chromatic scale patterns arranged in octave displacement. Basically two themes, the first beginning in m. 7 (note the melodic recall of the opening statement of *Allegro Barbaro*, Sz. 49), and the second a statement in seventh chords beginning in m. 24. Since the hands are almost always stretched to accommodate the wide intervals, one must exercise extreme caution not to overtax them. The prescribed MM marking of half note = 132 is in most cases unrealistic; the same musical results can be achieved in the 108–112 range. Frequent pedal changes or flutter pedals are recommended to enhance the legato effects called for. The fourth and fifth fingers of both hands will benefit considerably from this study.

No. 2. Andante sostenuto. (3' 5") T14 M14

Key center A. Compound arpeggio figures combined with two- and three-voice octaves and trills. Free form culminating in a cadenza passage marked "senza misura" and lacking bar lines. Draws stylistic parallels with Debussy's "pour les Arpèges composés" (*Etudes*, Vol. II), requiring the same delicacy of touch over a wide range of quick arpeggiations. Although this study is based generally on the interval of the third, an abundance of other interval relationships are presented, requiring great hand flexibility and the ability to execute evenness of sound in frequent fifth-finger to thumb crossovers. The two hands receive equal benefit from the arpeggio "exercise" and also take part in broken octaves and full chords in the "quasi cadenza" section.

No. 3. Rubato—Tempo giusto. (2' 5") T14 M14

Key center A. Loosely constructed ABA form, melodic and harmonic material based largely on a six-note motto (A, C-sharp, B-sharp, F-sharp, G-sharp, D), which is stated at the beginning and end. Basically a study for the left hand; its main difficulties are awkward and irregular configurations frequently above the middle-C range. Complex rhythmic setting with frequent meter changes (27 in all), offbeat accents, and double-stemmed melodic fragments. The B section is of a rather sentimental nature; its melody threads its way in the middle of arpeggio figures and intervals of the fifth in registers above and below. A difficult piece to make convincing, let alone effectively end the cycle.

Improvisations on Hungarian
Peasant Songs

Op. 20, Sz. 74
1920
T6–14 M11–14
10' 25"

Publication

Available separately:
B&H

No. 7, inscribed "à la mémoire de Claude Debussy," was published in the series "Tombeau de Claude Debussy" in *La Revue Musicale*, December 1, 1920; also included were works by other prominent composers of the period, including Stravinsky, Falla, and Satie.

Stuart Thyne gives a detailed analysis of the *Improvisations* in *Music and Letters*, January 1950, pp. 30–45.

Commentary

Bartók stated that, "In my *Eight Improvisations for Piano* I reached, I believe, the extreme limit in adding most daring accompaniments to simple folk tunes."[1] This work is a true masterpiece, the crowning achievement of Bartók's transcribing of folk material to the medium of the piano. It also indicates a strong tendency that continues in all his subsequent works, that of complete assimilation of the essential spirit of folk music into a unique and highly individualized compositional style. The cycle should be performed in its entirety, not only because of the contrasts and continuity of the musical material but also, as László Somfai points out, of the tonal interconnections of the work seen in the "attacca" grouping of the particular tonality spheres:

I–II	III–IV–V	VI	VI–VII	movements
C	G	E-flat	C	key center[2]

Movements

The folk texts are excerpted and paraphrased from the English translations in BBHU and personally acquired sources; complete texts in the original language appear in BBHU and SODO.

No. 1. Molto moderato. (1' 15") T6 M11

> My cousin made cakes which she took into the garden in a rose-colored cloth; her uncle followed her wearing a new cape and kissed her in the middle of the garden [Old Style melody].

Key center D; Dorian mode. Three variations plus coda. Use of major second, cross-relation thirds, then widely spaced chords of the tenth in the accompaniments. The arpeggio figurations are coloristic rather than functional, conveying a strumming effect. The melody in variation 2 should be distributed between the hands according to the direction of the stems (pointing up, right hand; pointing down, left hand). In m. 12, replay silently the left-hand chord so that the release of the pedal may clear the right-hand melody. Much sensitivity needed for this short but beautiful prelude.

No. 2. Molto capriccioso. (50") T12 M11

> J arrived in the evening for the congratulation of János; János, be in good health,
> I greet you in good health.

Key center C; Mixolydian mode. Four variations connected by interludes, progressing through the key centers of C, E, A-flat, and C respectively. Careful study needed of the subtle differences in melodic slur-staccato patterns in each variation, as well as variants of tempo (all MM markings) and mood. The transitions between variations need imaginative treatment to set up the character of the material following.

No. 3. Lento, rubato. (2' 15") T8 M14

> See the yellow-legged raven under a black cloud; stay you raven, take a message
> to my parents and to my betrothed; if they ask how I am, say I am ill, and that
> in the churchyard I long to find rest [Old Style melody].

Key center D, melodic material beginning and ending on D; Aeolian and Ionian modes. Three variations with interludes (mm. 16–17), progressing through key centers of D, F, and D. Mournful, despairing mood. Strumming accompaniment figure at very opening forecasts the coloristic effects of "Musiques Nocturnes" in *Out of Doors*, Sz. 81. Pay particular attention to the varied rhythmic treatment given to each figure (grace notes vs. triplets vs. sixteenth notes). Bartók uses this piece as an example of the third of three categories of folk music transcription, in which "the added composition-treatment attains the importance of an original work, and the used folk melody is only to be regarded as a kind of motto."[3]

No. 4. Allegretto scherzando. (40") T11 M12

> Along the sloping vineyards goes a little maid with her brother; the wind blows
> from the Danube and it always catches the poor folk [Mixed Style melody].

Key center G; Ionian, Mixolydian modes. Two variations with interlude and coda. While the melody in the first variation corresponds exactly to the original folk tune in contour and cadence structure (G–D, C–G), the melodic and cadential treatment in the second variation is significantly altered (F-flat–D-flat, A–G), a radical departure from Bartók's usual treatment of folk transcription. The cartwheel figures at the opening, a technique used by Debussy in "Feux d'artifice" (*Préludes*, Vol. II) might be thought of as portraying wind gusts (see text), and at least one analyst thought that they could be substitutes for microtones.[4] Lightness, wit, and a supple rhythmic sense are essential to the interpretation of this piece.

No. 5. Allegro [molto]. (45") T13 M11

Key center G; pentatonic melody. Five variations with transitions, the last presented as a development/coda section. The first twenty measures of the right hand should highlight the dominant D, considering the dissonant tones as super-imposed acciaccaturas. Be sure to emphasize the lower right-hand voice in variation 4 (beginning in m. 35); this technique of "joining in" at a different interval is a spontaneous trait in almost all kinds of folk or "sing-along" music making. The need for precise definition of the slur-staccato combinations in the tune and coordination of it with the offbeat accompaniments are the main difficulties.

No. 6. Allegro moderato, molto capriccioso. (1' 20") T13 M12

> When I was married I was given thirteen smocks, tralalala; I was given thirteen smocks, trala! [Old Style melody].
>
> Alas that I should embrace this old person; although very old, [he, she] needs my affection.

Key center E-flat; pentatonic melody. Introduction, three variations, and coda. Although the frequent black-key/white-key combinations suggest bi-tonality, the folk tune itself is deeply rooted in E-flat in all variations, the accompaniment material being merely ornamental. Some careful redistribution of fingerings can facilitate the awkward hand crossings in the introduction and coda. In variation 1 (beginning in m. 6), the confusing 5 against 4 rhythms (right and left hands respectively) are precisely notated in B&H, thus clarifying their proper vertical execution. A variety of idiomatic technical figurations is offered, such as cartwheel figurations (variation 2) and widely spaced tremolos (variation 3).

No. 7. Sostenuto, rubato. (1' 45") T9 M14

> Beli, my son Beli [Transylvanian lullaby].

Key center C; Aeolian mode. Two variations with episodic material and coda. Dedicated to the memory of Claude Debussy. Much use of mirror writing in the accompaniment chords and episodes. Note the clever melodic disguise in variation 2 (beginning in m. 16), where the melody is stated in octaves in the left hand, taken over by the right hand at m. 19, and rhythmically altered throughout. Measure 32 presents a sliding figuration suggestive of writing for the six-row *Janko* keyboard. This movement has a special beauty and poignancy and was described as "the most magnificent 'piano adagio' written since Schumann."[5]

No. 8. Allegro. (1' 35") T14 M12

> To plough in winter is hard work, one can hardly hold the plough; 'tis better to remain abed disporting with a young woman [Old Style melody].

Key center C; Dorian mode. Four variations with interludes progressing through tonal centers of B (C pedal), D (melodically altered), E (canon at the tritone), and C (extended for a brilliant close). As the text indicates, the setting is bold and lustful, with many opportunities for imaginative portrayal. This movement was used as an illustration, in one of Bartók's Harvard lectures of 1943, of one of his most elaborate settings of original folk material for piano.[6] As can be expected, difficulties are many and severe: awkward chordal configurations for both hands, octave leaps, extremes of dynamic change, and the need for precision and suppleness of movement.

Recordings

Hungaroton LPX 12333-B. *Bartók at the Piano*, Vol. I, 1981. Side 16, Band 2 (Nos. 1, 2, 6, 7, and 8), 1941.

Turnabout/Vox THS 65010. *Bartók Plays Bartók*. Side 2, Band 2 (Nos. 1, 2, 6, 7, and 8), 1941.

Hungaroton LPX 12334-B. *Bartók Plays and Talks*, Vol. II, 1981. Side 1, Band 10 (Nos. 4 and 5), 1932.

Although side-by-side comparisons of the 1932 and 1941 recordings are impossible because none of the movements are duplicated, one perceives a brisker and rhythmically more straightforward conception of the pieces in the earlier recording and a more ponderous and weightier approach in the later one. No. 1 receives a taut and intense melodic delivery with crystalline brightness in the upper-register seconds and thirds in the first two variations; in variation 3, the tops of the left-hand rolled chords are delayed sufficiently to give the appearance of a countermelody. No. 2 is played more heavily and seriously than one usually hears it, with less accelerando than indicated until the last variation. By contrast, Nos. 4 and 5 are given a more virtuosic treatment, with brisker tempos and more abandon. The "poco rubato" section of No. 6, marked slower than the beginning, is so light and capricious that it appears to be faster than its predecessor; although marked "sempre più pesante" at the very end, there is no ritard. The mannerism of rolling or staggering strategic chords, typical of nineteenth-century pianists, is quite prevalent in the performance of No. 7 but seems here to serve the function of delineating contrapuntal voices. No. 8 is a kaleidoscope of tempo and dynamic contrasts and is effectively presented as a true character piece rivaling the best of Schumann and Debussy.

Notes

1. BBES, p. 375.
2. Hungaroton SPLX 11337, Vol. VII, p. 9.
3. BBES, p. 352.
4. *Music and Letters*, January 1950, 38 (fn.).
5. UJFA, p. 190.
6. BBES, p. 375.

Dance Suite

Sz. 77
1925
T7-15 M9-14
15' 35"

Publication

Available separately:
UE
Transcribed by Bartók from the original orchestral version of the same name (also Sz. 77, 1923).

Commentary

The *Dance Suite* was written originally as a commissioned work for orchestra, along with Kodály's *Psalmus Hungaricus* and Dohnányi's *Festival Overture*, to celebrate the fiftieth anniversary of the merging, in 1873, of Pest, Buda, and Obuda into the city of Budapest. The director of UE suggested to Bartók that that he write a "not too difficult" transcription of the score for piano. Although the orchestral setting was a decided success, the piano version never became popular, and Bartók himself never played it.[1] Its world première was given in New York's Carnegie Hall in March 1945, and the performer, György Sándor, recalls that "Bartók had done considerable rewriting of the score for me, and he was present at the concert."[2] Despite the unavoidable technical awkwardnesses in this or any piano reduction from an orchestral score, the *Dance Suite* is eminently playable, the color possibilities endless, and the effort totally rewarding. It is of course essential to study the orchestral version of the work before undertaking the piano solo; comparison of the orchestra and piano scores reveals frequent instances where the dynamic level for the piano is at least one degree softer than that of the orchestra at a parallel place.

Movements

No. 1. Moderato. (3' 30") T14 M12

Key center G; contains Bartók's "first 'chromatic' melody" typifying Arabic folk style.[3] Freely composed with frequent changes of tempo and mood. Widely spaced chord formations, quick chordal leaps, and interlocking hands (mm. 14–20) requiring some redistribution. Sostenuto pedal can be used for sustained tones. The motive at mm. 76–79 becomes an important thematic element in No. 6. The "ossia" at mm. 99–101 hardly does justice to the climactic nature of the section and should be avoided.

Ritornell. Tranquillo (beginning at m. 120 of No. 1).

Although part of No. 1, this transition provides lyrical relief from it and the tempestuous No. 2. The same material acts as a bridge between Nos. 2 and 3 (Tranquillo) and Nos. 4 and 5 (Lento) and appears as part of No. 6 (Molto tranquillo). Melodic structure similar to an Old Style Hungarian folk tune. Each statement of the "Ritornell" is increasingly slower and more reminiscent. Requires control of widely spaced legato voicings, sustained harmonies, and light rhythmic offbeats in the lower voices.

No. 2. Allegro molto. (2' 10") T14 M11

Key center B-flat. Of Hungarian character and spirit.[4] Three-part form, each section developing a repeated minor-third slur motif. Compelling Stravinskian rhythmic drive, metric changes, sharp accents of all types. The chromatic glissandi at mm. 7, 20, 56, and 85, so effective on the trombones in the orchestral version, do not lend themselves well to the piano version, especially when set in octave displacement; the single-voice chromatic scale, middle-C range, would seem to suffice in all instances. Light as well as percussive touches are called for, considering the variety of dynamic levels.

No. 3. Allegro vivace. (2' 40") T13 M10

Key center B; pentatonic scale at opening, Lydian mode in middle section (beginning in m. 46). Combination of Hungarian, Romanian, and Arabic influences.[5] Festive atmosphere throughout. The A section, Hungarian in origin, presents a whimsical bagpipe melody that grows in vitality upon each repetition. The B section (beginning in m. 46), Romanian in origin, also depicts bagpipe music, with metric changes almost every measure. The C section (beginning in m. 95) is of a heroic nature and requires octave and chord-rebound facility. "Vivacissimo" coda based on the A material. The Arabic influence that Bartók speaks of is found in the chromatic scale melodies in mm. 31, 35, 40, and 111–121. Although this movement is perhaps the most pianistic of the set, there are many awkward places, such as quick alternations of single notes and octaves in the right hand, grace-note and glissando configurations, and other coloristic effects designed for orchestra.

No. 4. Molto tranquillo. (2' 30") T7 M14

Key center G. Widely spaced repeated chords alternating with ornamented melody in octaves. Based entirely on oriental or Arabic origins.[6] The same dualism of textures (chordal vs. linear) found in the second movement of *Piano*

Concerto No. 2, Sz. 95. The chordal statements do not exceed a *piano* dynamic, while the linear statements are indicated *p-f-p*. Metronome markings are faster than generally heard in performance, but changes in tempo should be proportionate to the basic tempo chosen. Measure 19 should read eighth note (*not* quarter note) = 132–144. Although this movement is technically the least difficult of the set, it offers challenges in sustaining the tranquil and hypnotic mood. The aesthetic is actually *non*-expression and avoidance of the *parlando-rubato* interpretation one normally associates with a folk style in slow tempo.

No. 5. Commodo. (55") T11 M9

Key center E. Described by Bartók as having a "primitive Romanian quality,"[7] although the narrow melodic range and repeated-note patterns suggest Arabic influences. Orchestration calls for muted strings and brass. Sostenuto pedal can be used on the first left-hand octave (E), depressed silently before the beginning of the movement and maintained until m. 18. Except for two *ff* outbursts at mm. 18 and 22, the prevailing dynamic level is *p-mp-p*, calling for delicate rhythmic control. Certain three-voice quartal chords (e.g., mm. 11 and 13) can be effectively reduced to two voices to facilitate smoothness of the triplet rhythms.

No. 6. Finale. Allegro (3' 50") T15 M14

Key centers C and G. Presents "a synthesis of . . . characteristics" found in the previous movements.[8] The general outline of thematic presentation of the preceding movements is as follows: m. 1: buildup of fourths as found in No. 5; m. 21: No. 2; m. 55: No. 3; m. 65: No. 5; m. 83: "trombone" motive of No. 6; m. 94: No. 2; m. 112: "Ritornell"; m. 120: original material; m. 164: No. 3. The difficulties in this movement are not much different or more complex than those in similar situations in the preceding ones; the real challenge is the successful assimilation of diverse elements into a unified whole and the sustaining of musical excitement over a large span of time and content. Suggested cuts in this movement are mm. 17 (after the fermata)–35 and mm. 149–159.

Notes

1. Hungaroton SPLX 11337, Vol. VII, p. 9.
2. *High Fidelity/Musical America*, September 1970, 28. The cuts that Bartók recommended are as follows: No. 2, mm. 60–85; No. 4, m. 28; and No. 6, mm. 17 (after the fermata)–35 and mm. 74–100. Most of them seem to have an adverse effect on the structural balance of the movements, except for those suggested for No. 6.
3. BBES, p. 379.
4. Ibid., p. 396; BBLE, p. 202.

5. BBLE, p. 202.
6. Ibid.
7. BBES, p. 396.
8. Ibid.

Sonata

Sz. 80
1926
T10-15+ M13-15
12' 45"

Publication

Available separately:
B&H
UE

Commentary

Sz. 80 is the only solo piano work by Bartók with the title *Sonata*. It is the first of a series of piano compositions written in 1926 that employ techniques of piano writing found only sporadically in his previous works. The most conspicuous of these is the martellato, or percussive, technique, which made its debut in *Allegro Barbaro*, Sz. 49, of 1911.[1] Other features of this new style include a strong, motoric rhythmic drive; emphasis on polyphonic rather than chordal writing; the frequent use of dissonant intervals of the second and the seventh; and cluster formations.

Although none of the musical material in the *Sonata* is based on original folk tunes, Bartók mentioned this work in particular as being influenced by the general spirit of folk music, where "in many cases themes or turns of phrases are deliberate or subconscious imitations of folk melodies or phrases. . . ."[2] From a technical and interpretive standpoint, the *Sonata* is one of Bartók's most difficult works for solo piano; Bartók himself had reservations about programming it for any but the most sophisticated audiences.[3] Only a pianist with a highly developed technique and a hand that can easily accommodate the stretch of a tenth should attempt this work.

Movements

No. 1. Allegro moderato. (4' 25") T15+ M13

Key center E. Sonata design with short development and full recapitulation. Small melodic range, most themes based on repeated-note motives. Consistent rhythmic drive, dissonance, and strong accents. Octaves, parallel grace-note figurations, hand stretches and contractions, leaps, sustained and moving voices in the same hand, and overlapping hand positions all contribute to the difficulty of the movement. Although the use of the sostenuto pedal for the tied notes in the development (mm. 140–166) might alleviate much of the awkwardness, it would also adversely weaken the inherent "struggle" of the technical situation and invalidate Bartók's own repeated-thumb fingerings (a similar situation is found in "Wrestling," *Mikrokosmos*, Sz. 107, No. 108). Strength and endurance are required, along with the ability to absorb the many rhythmic and melodic irregularities, especially in the development section.

No. 2. Sostenuto e pesante. (4' 45") T10 M15

Key center C. Ternary form with varied repeat of the first section. Repeated-note patterns form the melodic basis for this hypnotically sustained movement. Maintaining a legato counterpoint in four-voice textures is a major difficulty (see especially mm. 11–12), requiring careful exchange of hands in the inner voices. At m. 30, the "p subito" effect in the bottom D is best effected by lifting the key slightly without fully releasing it and applying pedal only after the softer dynamic is achieved. Triads spanning the interval of a ninth are frequently called for in the right hand, especially in the B section; they should always be blocked, never rolled. The low-register sixths on the first beats of mm. 49–51, which are out of keyboard range on most pianos, can be redistributed by playing the lower notes an octave higher; this will retain the chord sound and approximate the desired low-register sonority.

No. 3. Allegro molto. (3' 35") T15+ M13

Key center E. Theme (in B Mixolydian), seven variations, and coda, with vigorous episodic material between the variations. Difficulties include tone clusters, octaves, hand stretches and contractions, and leaps. At mm. 38–39 we find a particularly formidable example of the chordal leaps that occur frequently in the movement; also, at mm. 84 and 86, the right hand must play a seven-note cluster spanning a tenth, the thumb playing three keys at once! The repeated-thumb fingerings at the second episode (beginning in m. 111) are Bartók's own and suggest an unusually percussive touch that cannot be achieved with consecutive fingerings. At this point, the left-hand chords that cannot be blocked should be rolled as quickly and imperceptibly as possible. The "chirping" figurations[4] in the third and fourth variations (beginning in mm. 143 and 205) require clearly articulated statements of the two-note slur figurations. The coda material presents some of the most electrifying piano writing of the twentieth century. This movement is the most approachable of the three because of the folk-like melody of the main theme, the rich variety of color effects, and the idiomatic figurations in the variations and episodes.

Notes

1. Bartók himself admitted in 1927 that, although "the neutral character of the piano tone has been long recognized, . . . its inherent nature becomes really expressive only by means of the present tendency to use the piano as a percussion instrument" (BBES, p. 288).
2. Ibid., pp. 349–350.
3. BBLE, p. 227; *High Fidelity/Musical America*, September 1970, 28.
4. STEV, p. 134.

Out of Doors

Sz. 81
1926
T10-15+ M8-15
14' 45"

Publication

Available separately:
B&H
UE, as *Im Freien*

Commentary

Out of Doors is the first example of descriptive or representational music since the *Burlesques* of 1908–1911. Written at a time when Bartók was involved with editing keyboard works of Baroque and pre-Baroque composers, the cycle reflects

descriptive elements of some of the shorter character pieces of this period, especially those of the French claveciniste and the English virginalist composers; it
also continues the trend of Liszt and Debussy in using the piano as an instrument of sound portrayal. The sounds of primitive instruments in Nos. 1 and
3, the swaying aquatic motions in No. 2, and sounds of natural phenomena in
Nos. 4 and 5 are all duplicated as authentically as the resources of the piano
will permit. Although Nos. 4 and 5 are sometimes performed separately, the
cycle should be played as a complete unit and can easily be the major work on
a piano recital.

Movements

No. 1. With Drums and Pipes. Pesante. (1' 45") T11 M9
  Key center D (the true center, although the opening melody is in E). ABA
form, of which A represents the drum material and B (beginning in m. 41) the
more linear and lyrical woodwind material. Historical ties with the *galoubet* (re-
corder-type instrument) and the *tambourin* (a small side drum) of the thirteenth
century, the two instruments being played by one musician. The piece also
reflects dance music of eighteenth-century France played by pipe and *Tambour
de Basque* (see also Sz. 82, No. 8). Drum sounds are effectively portrayed by
superimposed upper-neighbor tones, giving the effect of clusters, but within a
deeply rooted tonal scheme. The B section offers the most difficulties, requiring a hand capable of blocking ninths (frequently alternating with single tones
a step above and below) and executing legato octaves. For the most effective
performance the percussiveness should always be kept in check; note that the
only time that the dynamic exceeds *f* is at mm. 104–105.

No. 2. Barcarolla. Andante. (2' 50") T10 M12
  Key center G. Six sections: introduction, principal theme on G, then on
D, a modulatory development section, a reprise of the introduction and principal theme on A, and a shift back to G at the end. Linear counterpoint
throughout, melodic minor-type scale figures and quartal harmonies. Unlike
comparable examples of the nineteenth century, by Mendelssohn, Chopin, or
Fauré, in which a consistent metric pulse is the rule, this piece undergoes no
fewer than 79 metric changes, portraying the irregular waves and currents that
a vessel would encounter. Difficult to memorize because of these irregularities.
Must maintain a virtually unbroken, almost legatissimo melodic fluidity
throughout, punctuated only by the staccato sixteenth notes, which occur with
the sustained octaves. In B&H, there is a misprint at m. 83: the pedal tone
should read F instead of A.

No. 3. Musettes. Moderato. (2' 55") T12 M13

Key center D. Structure largely determined by the tonal levels, which for the most part correspond to the circle of fourths: A, D, G, C, and D, with episodic material presented twice on G. Reflects the type of bagpipe music in the court of Louis XIV, as depicted in some of the keyboard music of the clavecinistes, the trios of many of the optional movements in J. S. Bach's keyboard suites, and numerous other examples by Bartók himself. Many super-imposed dissonances, trill figurations, and bellows-like slur effects. The piece can sound blatantly unmusical unless extreme care is taken to observe every tempo and dynamic change (which in some places can occur every measure). The trill and tremolo figures are difficult, especially when they are begun from a chord position, when an important tone is indicated in large print, and when they are presented in parallel fourths. The musical effect should always be comparable to the stress-release feeling of the two-note slur, avoiding any kind of an accent on its release.

No. 4. Musiques Nocturnes. Lento. (5' 10") T10 M15

Key center G. Loose rondo form (ABACABA), the A sections supplying the atmospheric semitonal figurations, and B and C the melodic material. According to Bartók's son Béla, Jr., the present example "took its origin from [the vicinity of Vésztö]; in it my father perpetuated the concert of the frogs heard in peaceful nights on the Great Plain."[1] Similar effects of musical illustration can be found in Couperin's "Les Abeilles" (The Bees) and "Le Moucheron" (The Mosquito), Ravel's "Noctuelles" (in *Miroirs*), Bartók's "From the Diary of a Fly" (*Mikrokosmos*, Sz. 107, No. 142), and the middle section of the second movement of *Piano Concerto No. 3*, Sz. 119.

The semitone and its inversion, the major seventh, are the prevailing intervals in the piece and are similar in use to the whole tone in Debussy's "Voiles" (*Préludes*, Vol. I). This example is one of the most original, colorful, and poignant in this period of Bartók's writing, despite the heavy dissonance and seeming lack of tonality. Actually, upon close analysis, one finds a very strict adherence to conventional harmonic practice, every semitonal dissonance clearly conforming to the basic tonality in one way or another. The random and fragmentary presentation of material, in keeping with the unpredictablity of nature, makes this work extremely difficult to memorize, but it gives free reign to the performer's imagination and sense of fantasy.

No. 5. The Chase. Presto. (2' 5") T15+ M8

Key center F. Six-part form; consisting of a short introduction, followed by five sections, similar in material but always increasing in texture, technical complexity, and intensity. Precedents of hunting music are found in the Italian *Caccia* of the fourteenth century, the English *Catch* of the seventeenth and eighteenth centuries, and the piano etudes of Liszt ("Mazeppa," "Wilde Jagd," and "La Chasse"). The galloping ostinato figure, in which the leading tone,

E, is accented (F, G-sharp, B, C-sharp, and E), expands at each section by a redistribution of the tones in the figure. The characteristic techniques in the melodic material consist of martellato repeated notes and intervals (up to a ninth) interspersed with scalar melodic fragments. From the standpoint of technique and endurance, especially for the left hand, this movement could easily be the most demanding in Bartók's entire output; it is said that Bartók himself had considerable difficulty maintaining his prescribed MM marking of quarter note = 144–160, and it would be foolhardy for anyone else to try to approach this speed. It is, nonetheless, one of the best left-hand "etudes" in the piano repertoire and an enormously effective concert piece.

Note

1. CROW, p. 151.

Nine Little Piano Pieces

Sz. 82
1926
T5–12 M5–11
14' 45"

Publication

Available separately:
B&H (Vols. I, II, and III also published separately)
UE

Commentary

This three-volume collection offers an attractive and novel array of contrapuntal studies (Vol. I), character pieces (Vol. II), and a brilliant concert piece (Vol. III). None of the examples in this set have achieved much popularity, most likely because of the contrast between their miniature proportions and fragmentary nature and the more monumental character of other piano works of

1926 and the *Mikrokosmos*, Sz. 107. They are nonetheless attractive recital repertoire, especially the individual pieces of Vols. II and III.

Movements

Volume I: Four Dialogues

The strengths of the pieces in this volume lie more in their contrapuntal in-
genuity than in their performability. They use, almost exclusively, two-voice
counterpoint of the type found in Vol. IV of *Mikrokosmos*, Sz. 107. Although
the Bach inventions are said to have been influential in the writing of this
volume, the contrapuntal treatment reflects more the freely written counterpoint
of the pre-Bach keyboard composers, especially those of seventeenth-century
Italy.

No. 1. Moderato. (1' 25") T5 M6

Key center E. Two voices in counterpoint throughout, except for octave
doublings near the end. The emphasis in this example is on canonic imitation,
alternating between the sixth, the fifth, and finally the third. The points of imitation progress from the whole note, to the half note, and finally to the quarter
note, creating a gradual stretto effect.

No. 2. Andante. (1' 10") T5 M6

Key center A; Dorian mode. Two- and three-voice counterpoint. Theme
and three variations, interspersed with episodes. A good study in legato phrasing. The final variation can be quite effective coloristically if the damper pedal
is used to sustain the low A, but the sostenuto pedal can be used as well. The
"ossia" version (beginning at m. 26) is not really a simplification and does not
supply the color effects found in the original.

No. 3. Lento. (1' 35") T5 M6

Key center C. Free two-voice counterpoint, occasionally extending to three
voices for harmonic enrichment. Highly chromatic melodic treatment with frequent cross-relation melodic retracing reminiscent of "Barcarolla" from *Out of
Doors*, Sz. 81, written in the same year. The two main cadences emphasizing
the dominant and tonic of C display a curious combination of trill and *Schleifer*
(slide) in contrary motion.

No. 4. Allegro vivace. (1' 40") T7 M6

Key center E-flat. Free two-voice counterpoint, the main material being the
opening subject in the upper voice. The given MM marking of quarter note
= 152 is almost unplayable; 120 would seem more realistic. The rhythmic
figurations are pianistically awkward, and fingerings should be devised to avoid
thumbs on the black keys. Accents need much hand and wrist support.

Volume II

This volume could be presented as a self-contained suite of dances, suitable for a pianist with a good imagination and sense of tonal color but whose technique is not up to the demands of *Out of Doors*, Sz. 81.

No. 5. Minuetto. Moderato. (1' 40") T4 M7

Key center A. Basically three-voice homophonic textures. Does not reflect the grace and charm of the Baroque minuet, but has a sinister, stagnant quality with frequent repeated notes in lower registers. Stevens refers to it as "almost a caricature of the minuet style."[1] A subtle sense of satire could make this piece effective.

No. 6. Lied. Allegro. (50") T9 M5

Key center A. Introduction using left-hand clusters and right-hand staccato-legato combinations, followed by two variations of a folk-like tune stated in simple two-voice counterpoint and then combined with the cluster figurations of the introduction. An attractive and performable piece, one of the most transparent in the entire set.

No. 7 Marcia Delle Bestie (March of the Animals). Comodo. (1' 40") T7 M5

Key center B-flat. Cluster effects alternating with a theme that undergoes continual development. The juxtaposition of the tempo marking "comodo" and the opening dynamic "marcato f" seems contradictory until one realizes that this is the composer's way of tempering one's impulses toward percussive playing. Similar in character to the bear dances in *Ten Easy Pieces*, Sz. 39, and the *Sonatina*, Sz. 55. Only occasionally does the dynamic level reach *ff*; accents should be played lightly enough to give the effect of an animal parade in miniature.

No. 8. Tambour de Basque (Tambourin). Allegro molto. (1') T8 M5

Key center G. Quartal quasi-cluster chords with occasional melody. The *Tambour de Basque* is simply the familiar tambourin (compare the example of the same title by Rameau). The same stylization of instrumental sonorities in this piece is found in "Drums and Pipes" and "Musettes" from *Out of Doors*. Although drumlike effects dominate the piece, the same care should be taken to keep the accents light and in proportion to the given dynamic.

Volume III

Not really a volume, since it contains only one piece.

No. 9. Preludio—All Ungherese (Prelude in the Hungarian Style). Molto moderato—Allegro non troppo, molto ritmico. (3' 45") T12 M11

Key center G-sharp. An extended fantasy-type piece with elements of variation. The introduction presents the main theme rather inconspicuously arrayed and surrounded by episodes and transitions. When the "Allegro" section enters, the main theme takes on a life of its own and undergoes five transformations that continually intensify in dynamic, texture, and speed. A good repeated-note technique, octave technique, and endurance are prime requisites. The *Preludio* is brilliantly effective and can stand on its own in performance and even end a program or group of miscellaneous pieces.

Recordings

Hungaroton LPX 12326-B. *Bartók at the Piano*, Vol. I, 1981. Side 2, Bands 4a (No. 6) and 4b (No. 8), c. 1936.

Bartók BRS 903, c. 1950/1936.

Hungaroton LPX 12333-B. *Bartók at the Piano*, Vol. I, 1981. Side 16, Band 3 (No. 9), 1941.

Continental 4007 (Set 102), c. 1949, c. 1941.

Vox-Turnabout THS 65010. *Bartók Plays Bartók*. Side 1, Band 3 (No. 9), 1941.

In No. 6, the opening "Allegro" is played with strict adherence to accents, staccatos, and note values; the "meno mosso" is weighty and not at all delicate; the "Più mosso" begins with more elegance and lavish rubato effects and builds very gradually to a brilliant conclusion. No. 8 is played considerably faster than the prescribed MM marking, but it is only mildly percussive, suggesting an instrument of muted timbre. The rather enigmatic "molto moderato" section of No. 9 is vitalized by the composer's keen attention to the many dynamic changes that occur. From the "allegro non troppo" section (beginning in m. 52) to the end of the piece, one cannot help but be swept away by the gradual but compelling dynamic escalation, effected primarily by the step-by-step increase in tempo, dynamic, and pedal application over a span of 80 measures.

Note

1. STEV, p. 137.

Three Rondos on Folk Tunes

Sz. 84
No. 1, 1916; Nos. 2 and 3, 1927
T9–11 M10–11
6' 55"

Publication

Available separately:
B&H
UE
Transcribed by Pál Bodon for orchestra (1928).

Commentary

This set, based on seven Slovakian folk tunes, presents vivid side-by-side examples of the stylistic and pianistic differences in Bartók's writing from the mid-1910s to the mid-1920s. It was originally entitled *Rhapsodies*, but the rondo form was probably chosen to accommodate more than one folk tune in a single piece, by means of primary and secondary themes. This arrangement can be viewed as a structural alternative to the binary and ternary forms of the Romanian folk settings of 1915. Because of their similarity in structure and content, the *Rondos* can be performed individually, or No. 1 can be paired with either No. 2 or No. 3.

Movements

The folk texts are excerpted and paraphrased from personally acquired English translations; complete texts in the original language appear in BBSL (Vols. I and II) and SODO.

No. 1. Andante; Allegro molto; Allegro giocoso. (2' 15") T10 M11

[A theme] Hey, Mariena, hey! Where have you been?
Behind the valleys and mountains, washing my feet.

[B theme] In front of the stream, behind the stream, there is black [fertile] soil.

[C theme] I had a wife from Orava who had a big belly; haj-kon, tid-li-kon, tid-li-tid-li, tid-li-kon [nonsense refrain].

Key center C (A theme) with key changes to E (B theme), and A-flat (C theme). ABACA form. The most transparent and most often performed piece of the set. The benign simplicity of the three statements of the A theme is offset by two energetic and technically difficult episodes. Close attention must be paid to the intricacies of the slur-staccato combinations throughout, especially in the first episode (B theme, beginning in m. 43), where difficulties are posed by two- and three-note slurs, coordination problems, and the rhythmic complications of grace notes and offbeat syncopations in the left hand. Parallel triads in the right hand require a good chord-rebound technique. Remember that in its second appearance in m. 138, the melody is in the thumb.

No. 2. Vivacissimo; Allegro non troppo; Allegro assai. (2' 20") T11 M11

[A theme: no text.]

[B theme] Hey, when we return from the wedding, then we know that she is ours; when we look in her eyes, then we are sure that we have her.

[C theme: no text.]

Key center D; Mixolydian mode (A and B themes) and F; Lydian mode (C theme). ABACABA form. Nos. 2 and 3, written eleven years later than No. 1, are more contrapuntal and structurally more complex, and they use techniques that reflect the martellato and dissonant style of 1926–1927 as opposed to the more transparent folk-inspired writing of 1915. In this example, the A theme is presented as a heavily accented drone, and the two contrasting themes (B and C) are more lyrical and lighter. Difficulties include the coordination of sustained and moving voices in the same hand and the same rebound technique required in No. 1. The strident dissonances in the statements of the A theme can be held in check by emphasizing the melodic voice.

No. 3. Allegro molto; Meno mosso; Molto tranquillo. (2' 20") T9 M10

[A theme]: A little girl wandered up and down the hills; she didn't go [text incomplete].

[B theme: no text.]

Key center F; Lydian mode (A theme) and A; Mixolydian mode (B theme). xAxAxBxA-x form, x acting as percussive and syncopated bridge material separating the more lyrical A and B themes; requires rapid readjustments in touch and mood. The cluster-type accompaniment chords at the first statement of A (beginning in m. 27) require a flexible hand; when they are rolled at m. 35, a turning hand motion works better than finger articulation. Pay particular attention to the subtle touch differences in the three statements of the B theme (beginning in m. 54). The alternative octave doublings ("ossia" at mm. 35 and 130) could well be considered for tonal variety and balance with the thick accompaniment patterns. More appealing than No. 2.

Recordings

Hungaroton LPX 12326-B. *Bartók at the Piano*, Vol. I, 1981. Side 2, Band 3 (No. 1), 1936.
Bartók BRS 903, c. 1950/1936.
Hungaroton LPX 12333-B. *Bartók at the Piano*, Vol. I, 1981. Side 16, Band 1b (No. 1), 1941.

Continental CLP 101, c. 1949/1941.

Turnabout/Vox THS 65010. *Bartók Plays Bartók.* Side 1, Band 1 (No. 1).

The 1936 and 1941 recordings of No. 1 are almost carbon copies of each other, with the earlier one being somewhat more refined. In both instances, one notices clear and precise delineation of phrases and slurs and lavish rubato in the statements of the A theme, suggesting something other than naïve children's music. In the first episode, the composer plays all the "ossia" octave doublings, enhancing greatly the bravura quality of the section. The three-measure grand pause (beginning in m. 91) is observed with metronomic precision. The "meno forte" section of the second episode (beginning in m. 110) is played so lightly it could well be described as "piano, scherzando." The general impression upon hearing both performances is that this piece can indeed have qualities of a rhapsody rather than that of a predictable rondo.

Petite Suite

Sz. 105

1936

T7–12 M6–11

6' 20"

Publication

Available separately:

B&H

UE

Transcribed by Bartók for piano from Nos. 28, 32, 38, 43, 16, and 36 of *Forty-Four Duos* for two violins, Sz. 98 (1931).

For reasons unknown, the "Walachian Dance" (No. 2 in UE) does not appear in some issues of B&H, although its musical value seems to be equal to that of the others.

Commentary

Forty-Four Duos could be considered a string-instrument counterpart to certain of Bartók's piano sets, such as *For Children*, Sz. 42, and *The First Term at the Piano*, Sz. 53, in which "folk tunes are used predominately as thematic material . . . written with pedagogical purposes."[1] *Petite Suite* is considerably more difficult than these works, primarily because of the pianistic awkwardness encountered with the transfer of medium. Unlike previously composed folk-music cycles for piano, *Petite Suite* draws upon folk tunes from a variety of regions and nationalities. It is of course advisable to become familiar with the violin version of each piece for coloristic and interpretive perspective.

Movements

The folk texts are excerpted and paraphrased from the English translations in BBHU, BBRO (Vol. I), and personally acquired sources; complete texts in their original languages appear in BBHU, BBRO (Vol. I), and SODO.

No. 1. Slow Air (No. 28, "Sadness," in Sz. 98). Lento, poco rubato. (2' 5") T7 M11

> My steed's copper horseshoe is shining; the daughter of the innkeeper of Madaras is so peevish and her shoes so ragged; she costs me much, but all in vain [Hungarian folk tune].

Key center A; Dorian and Mixolydian modes. Two variations preceded and followed by an ostinato figure that serves as a backdrop for most of the piece. Main difficulty is expressive delivery of legato octaves and full chords. The only piece of the set in the Old Style.

No. 2. Walachian Dance (No. 32, "Dancing Song," in Sz. 98). Allegro giocóso. (45") T9 M6

> Hey, proud [peacock], don't shake [your feathers] too much [Romanian folk tune].

Key center D; pentatonic melody. Two variations and coda. Octave slurs abound, requiring a large hand and agile thumb technique. The offbeat left-hand accompaniment figures at m. 13 are pizzicato in the *Duo* version; Bartók curiously indicates "(Ped.)" for the pianist. Some performances will omit this piece because of its absence in B&H.

No. 3. Whirling Dance (No. 38 in Sz. 98). Allegro. (40") T11 M6

> [Violin tune of Romanian origin.]

Key center D; Lydian mode. Two variations and coda. Four voices widely spaced, causing problems where legato playing is called for. The variation at m. 17 is in a crossed-hands formation for four measures, causing problems of coordination. A joyous mood prevails.

No. 4. Quasi pizzicato (No. 43, "Pizzicato," in Sz. 98). Allegretto. (1' 5") T10 M7

I'll see no swallows in winter; now I'll kill a brace of cockerels, eat their hearts and livers, and kiss the lips of my beloved [Hungarian folk tune, Mixed Style melody].

Key center G; Lydian mode. Five variations. Figurations and textures change with each variation. The most difficult technical situation occurs in the first four measures: widely spaced rolled chords surround the tune in the center, which is transferred from one hand to the other. Playing the rolls as quickly as possible, almost as blocks (as written in the *Duo* version), will help solve the difficulty of adapting a string technique to the keyboard.

No. 5. Ukrainian (Little Russian) Dance (No. 16, "Burlesque," in Sz. 98). Allegretto. (50") T10 M7

[Ukrainian folk song.]

Key center B-flat; Ionian mode. Canonic imitation. Three variations. The piano version is more interesting than the *Duo* version because where the latter has repeat signs, the former has the repeats written out in elaborated form. Entire piece built on offbeat slurs, some involving octaves and chords of as many as four voices. Pizzicato effects. The octave glissando at m. 36 is best replaced by the "ossia" above; it is easier and musically more effective.

No. 6. Bagpipes (No. 36, "The Bagpipe," in Sz. 98). Allegro molto in Sz. 98, but no tempo marking in the piano version; both have the same MM marking. (55") T12 M6

[Bagpipe tune of Romanian origin.]

Key center G; combination of Lydian and Mixolydian modes. Three sections, all built on drone-bass accompaniment and melody with rhythm of two sixteenth notes and an eighth. The *Duo* version has a variation option that alters the rhythm of the drone and adds acciaccaturas to the melody. The piano version retains the same melodic ornamentation but not the rhythmic alteration. As in No. 5, the piano version supplies varied repetitions for some sections for which only repeat signs are indicated for the violins. Difficulties lie in structural memory and in the octave acciaccaturas resolving to single notes.

Recordings

Hungaroton LPX 12326-33. *Bartók at the Piano*, Vol. I. Side 2, Band 4 (No. 6), c. 1941; Side 15, Band 5, (complete) c. 1941.

Vox-Turnabout THS 65010. *Bartók Plays Bartók*, 1974. Side 1, Band 2.

In No. 1, the ostinato sections beginning and ending the movement are played in strict tempo. The folk tune (beginning in m. 8) has considerable agogic stress on the first eighth note of the prevailing "lassú" rhythm. The second part of No. 2 ("Walachian Dance") never arrives at the "Tempo I" indicated at m. 15, being almost a reflective digression from the opening twelve measures. No. 3 maintains a brisk strict-tempo pace throughout, while No. 4 is slower than Bartók's prescribed MM marking of quarter note = 116, giving it a somewhat reticent quality. Much flexibility of tempo takes place in No. 5, the "più tranquillo" sections being considerably held back. The drone effects in No. 6 serve precisely the function they were assigned, namely, a light backdrop that should not dominate the sound effect. The ornamental effects are stunning.

Note

1. BBES No. 47.

Mikrokosmos

Sz. 107
1926–1937

Publication

Available separately:
B&H (Nos. 142 and 146 also published separately)
EMB, as *Mikrokozmosz*

Nos. 113, 69, 135, 123, 127, 145, and 146 transcribed by Bartók for two pianos, four hands (*Seven Pieces from "Mikrokosmos,"* B&H). Nos. 139, 137, 117, 142, 102, 151, and 153, with No. 3 of *Three Hungarian Folk Tunes*, Sz. 66, as prelude transcribed for orchestra by Tibor Serly (*Suite From "Mikrokosmos,"* B&H). Nos. 139, 102, 108, 116, and 142 transcribed for string quartet by Tibor Serly (*Five Pieces from "Mikrokosmos,"* B&H). Selected examples transcribed by Benjamin Suchoff for two clarinets (*23 Progressive Clarinet Duos from "Mikrokosmos,"* B&H).

Mikrokosmos has been the subject for a multitude of articles, theses, dissertations, and monographs. Perhaps the most outstanding reference dealing exclusively with the collection is Benjamin Suchoff's *Guide to Bartók's Mikrokosmos* [SUGU]. This book is not only indispensable reading for the student and teacher of the *Mikrokosmos* but also an important primary reference. It quotes the composer himself about many of the pieces, thus providing further insights into Bartók's musical and pedagogical outlook. It includes background material to the *Mikrokosmos* (Preface); a brief but thorough biographical sketch of the composer (Chapter 1); an analysis of the work as a whole with special regard to rhythm, tonality, structure, general educational theory, and piano pedagogy; a digest of Bartók's own ideas on piano teaching, performance, and musicianship; and a complete inventory of touch forms, expression markings, tempo markings, dynamic markings, and accents that Bartók prescribed for the *Mikrokosmos* and his other piano works (Chapters 2 and 3). Each piece is accompanied by a description of the technical and musical requirements, Bartók's own comments, and suggestions for performance. An attempt will be made in the following analyses to supplement, rather than duplicate, the information found in the Suchoff *Guide*.

Commentary

Few composers since J. S. Bach have been as successful as Bartók in presenting an encyclopedic assemblage of material that addresses itself equally to the development of keyboard skills and the summarization of contemporary compositional techniques. Fifty years after its completion, the *Mikrokosmos* is considered the most notable keyboard collection of its kind in the twentieth century, comparable only to such monumental predecessors as the etudes of Chopin and the *Well-Tempered Clavier* of Bach.

In a lecture given on several American college campuses in 1940 and 1941, Bartók described the purpose of the *Mikrokosmos* in the following manner:

> My idea was to write piano pieces intended to lead the students from the very beginning and through the most important technical and musical problems of the first years, to a certain higher degree. This determined programme involves a very strict proceeding: there must be no gaps in the succession of the technical problems which have to follow each other in a very logical order.[1]

Bartók also refers to the *Mikrokosmos* as "a synthesis of all the musical and technical problems which were treated and in some cases only partially solved" in his earlier piano works.[2] This explains to some extent the almost exclusive use of original material and the de-emphasis on folk-tune transcription in the collection; according to Bartók, "it would have been quite impossible to find folk melodies for every technical or musical problem" confronting the pianist.[3]

This six-volume set progresses from the most elementary teaching pieces to the most advanced virtuoso material, offering at the same time a wide variety of styles and idioms representative of most of the major composers past and present. In his commentary about the individual examples, Bartók is quite generous in his acknowledgment of influences from Couperin and Bach to Gershwin and Prokofieff. Tibor Serly claims that "no treatise or textbook has ever been written that so tellingly reveals the story of the development of musical styles as these brief . . . sketches."[4] Melodic and chordal structures, modes, intervals, rhythms, and patent pianistic textures are all illustrated, as well as folk idioms, dance forms, variation forms, and examples of musical description. It is difficult to conceive of a more comprehensive and richly varied collection than the *Mikrokosmos*.

Although the collection attempts to present a consistent progression of difficulty in its 153 selections, Bartók did not insist that they be played or learned in strict numerical order. This latitude is manifested in his own recording of some of the pieces, where much shuffling of the numerical sequence is found, even in "Six Dances in Bulgarian Rhythm" (Nos. 148–153), which is usually performed as a self-contained unit. He allowed the teacher a certain amount of freedom and responsibility in assigning pieces appropriate to the individual student's needs, level, and abilities; in inventing exercises to correspond with particular technical difficulties in the pieces; and in devising practice variants such as sight reading, transposition, and ensemble situations. The examples are not always easy to teach or to comprehend, but they are continually challenging and rewarding once teachers realize that their analytical "homework" is as important as their students' practicing.

Movements

The folk texts in the *Mikrokosmos* are excerpted and paraphrased from the English translations in BBHU and personally acquired sources; complete texts in the original language appear in BBHU, SODB, and B&H. Comments in quotation marks preceding individual pieces are Bartók's, as reported in SUGU.

Volume I: Nos. 1–36
T1–4 M1–3
20' 12" (All the timings in this collection are Bartók's own and generally correspond to his MM markings.)

Six Unison Melodies: Nos. 1–6
The main purpose of these rudimentary studies is to foster legato touch, balanced hand and arm position, basic posture, and discreet delineation of phrases. Rests appear in two examples (Nos. 1 and 6) and should be precisely observed along with the note values preceding. With the exception of No. 3, the hands are spaced two octaves apart to provide for a better sense of equilibrium at the keyboard. The melodic ranges, all in a fixed five-finger position, and the basic note values are indicated in small pentachord notation above each piece. Only beginning fingerings are indicated so that note rather than number reading is enforced at the outset.

In "Teaching with *Mikrokosmos*," Ylda Novik suggests that since most of the pieces in the earlier volumes lie in a five-finger position, they "lend themselves quite naturally to transposition to all twelve pitches" and will improve the student's sight reading through development of "a sense of direction and inter-

val at the keyboard."[5] Approaches other than transposition can also be applied
to these early examples, such as transposition of one hand only; canonic imitation; mirror counterpoint; and experimentation with different touches, phrasings, and dynamic effects.   Since all the examples in Vol. I and some in
subsequent volumes are in five-finger position (i.e., the fingers of each hand
play a pentachord, with tones a step apart), any change of hand position involves a transposition of the pentachord rather than an extension of the hand.

No. 1. (20") T1 M1
  Key center C. Parallel motion two octaves apart. Two phrases of equal
length. Legato touch throughout.

Nos. 2a and b. (20" each) T1 M1
  Key center C (a) and A (b). Parallel motion two octaves apart. Two phrases
of equal length. Legato touch throughout.

No. 3. (30") T1 M1
  Key center D. Begins on the fifth scale degree. Parallel motion one octave
apart.   Four phrases of equal length, varying note values.   Legato touch
throughout.

No. 4. (20") T1 M1
  Key center C; major mode. Begins on the seventh degree. Two phrases of
equal length, varying note values. Parallel motion two octaves apart. Legato
touch throughout.

No. 5. (30") T1 M1
  Key center A; minor mode. Five phrases of unequal length (3 + 3 + 2 + 2
+ 3 mm.), varying note values. Parallel motion two octaves apart. Legato
touch throughout.

No. 6. (20") T1 M1
  Key center G; major mode. Three phrases of unequal length (4 + 2 + 3
mm.), varying note values. Parallel motion two octaves apart. Legato touch
throughout. Quarter rest on the downbeat gives feeling of a syncopation.

No. 7. Dotted Notes. (30") T1 M1
  Key center E; Phrygian mode. Four phrases of unequal length (4 + 3 + 4 +
3 mm.), varying note values. Parallel motion one octave apart. Legato touch
throughout. A study not only in the conventional dotted rhythm (dotted half
and quarter note), but also in the inverted dotted rhythm (quarter note and
dotted half), a rhythmic pattern typical of Hungarian folk music. A rhythmic
companion piece to No. 28.

No. 8. Repetition. (30") T1 M1
  Key center E; Aeolian mode. Two phrases, the second an inversion of the

first. Introduction of short three- to five-note slurs and repeated notes, which should be played as legato as possible. The sharp in the key signature of the treble clef is on the first space instead of its usual position on the top line; this was meant as a visual aid to line up the accidental with the F-sharps in the piece. The first piece in the set to introduce change of hand position.

No. 9. Syncopation. (35") T1 M1

Key center C. Irregular phrasing (4 + 3 mm., 4 + 3 mm.) and half notes tied over the bar line to quarter notes to produce the syncopated effect. Parallel motion one octave apart. Bartók suggests that the effect of syncopation should involve some energetic gesture such as foot tapping or head nodding on the suspended downbeats.[6] A rhythmic companion piece to No. 27.

No. 10. With Alternate Hands. (40") T2 M1

Key center D; key signature of A-flat, which suggests a kind of Locrian mode (tritone from 1 to 5). Irregular phrases presented in strict canonic imitation; the first piece of the set to depart from simultaneous parallel motion between the hands. Coordination problem of attack–release rather than counterpoint, since the melodic statements alternate with each other rather than overlap.

No. 11. Parallel motion. (27") T2 M1

Key center G; Mixolydian mode. Four phrases of equal length. Five-finger position. MM marking indicates a faster tempo than in earlier examples. For the first time the parallel motion is not an octave apart, but in tenths; it resolves to the octave at the end. Because the left hand is in E Phrygian, the feeling of G is not realized until the final cadence, causing a somewhat bitonal effect. Similar in content and difficulty to No. 1 of *The First Term at the Piano*, Sz. 53.

No. 12. Reflection. (25") T2 M1

Key center D; Dorian mode. Irregular phrasing and meter change. Five-finger position in symmetrical rather than parallel motion. Somewhat easier to coordinate than the previous parallel-motion examples, largely because of the natural tendency of the hands to mirror each other. A slight digression from the strict inversion in the last two measures to provide for a cadential effect.

No. 13. Change of Position. (30") T2 M1

Key center C; major mode. Structure of AABA. In five-finger position but involves hand position change, the first instance of this in the set. Good for developing hand position change without looking at the keyboard; the rests between the changes help to facilitate the operation. A companion piece to No. 17.

No. 14. Question and Answer. (40") T2 M1

Key center D; Dorian mode. Irregular phrase structure presented in an antecedent–consequent arrangement. Five-finger position transposed.

No. 15. Village Song. (25") T2 M1

Key center D; Mixolydian and major modes. Irregular phrase structure presented in much the same manner as in No. 13. Five-finger position transposed. The first example to have a descriptive rather than a technical title. Phrase structure outlines that of a typical Hungarian folk tune (AABBA). Some rather awkward finger coordinations with the C-sharps.

No. 16. Parallel Motion and Change of Position. (45") T2 M1

Key center C; major mode. Irregular phrase structure. Five-finger position transposed. The hand-position changes in this example are more difficult than those preceding, mainly because at first the hands play parallel counterpoint a tenth apart, then a thirteenth apart, and back to a tenth apart. The change of interval requires the hands to go different distances to find the new notes.

No. 17. Contrary Motion. (30") T2 M1

Key center C; major mode with raised fourth (Lydian) in lower voice. Phrase and melodic structure the same as in No. 13 but presented in mirror formation. The cross-relation between the F and the F-sharps is nothing new; according to Bartók, one can find similar instances in the counterpoint of J. S. Bach.[7] A good exercise for fingers 4 and 5 of the left hand.

Four Unison Melodies

Although Nos. 18–21 continue the trend of two-voice parallel motion an octave apart, they introduce intervals of the third and the fourth within the phrase. This is an advance over the previous examples, which presented only stepwise intervals within the phrase. Also for the first time, exercises are presented (Appendix, Nos. 1a–f) that parallel the difficulties encountered in the pieces.

No. 18. (20") T1 M1

Key center D; minor mode. Two phrases of five measures each. Legato touch throughout.

No. 19. (30") T2 M1

Key center C; major mode. Irregular phrase structure. Beginning fingerings for the first two phrases are 2 and 4, causing some awkwardness. The last phrase is extended by an augmentation of note values, providing an example of a built-in ritard.

No. 20. (40") T2 M1

Key center G; major mode. Irregular phrase structure. Difficulties similar to those of No. 19, presenting angular interval combinations. Whole and half rests.

No. 21. (22") T2 M1

Key center A; minor mode. Irregular phrase structure, some slurs. Introduction of the accent (>) and the separation sign (|), the latter indicating some break in sound between the phrases. The accents should be light, but with enough sound to avoid an agogic stress on the half note following (the same principle could be applied to Nos. 13 and 17).

No. 22. Imitation and Counterpoint. (28") T2 M2
(The exercises [Appendix, Nos. 2a and b] present inverted counterpoint of the type encountered in Nos. 22–25.)
  Key center G; Mixolydian mode. Irregular phrasing, ranging from lengths of two to eight measures. Five-finger position, canonic imitation at the sixth. For the first time in the set a dynamic (f) is introduced, which should be modified somewhat from common practice to suit the lean two-voice texture. Similar in content and difficulty to No. 3 of *The First Term at the Piano*, Sz. 53.

No. 23. Imitation and Inversion. (30") T2 M2
  Key center D. Four phrases of equal lengths presented in a quasi-imitation setting. The meaning of "inversion" is not the conventional one and is explained by Bartók in the Notes at the end of the volume. The technical and musical demands are much the same as for No. 22.

No. 24. Pastorale. (35") T2 M3
  Key center D; Lydian Mode. Three phrases of varying lengths (6 + 9 + 6 mm.). The first full-page example that stresses sustaining long legato lines. Introduction of the p dynamic. Voices should be practiced separately so that the expressive value of each may be fully realized.

No. 25. Imitation and Inversion. (57") T2 M3
  Key center B; non-diatonic mode because of the C-sharp in the key signature (closest to Locrian). Two sections of two phrases each, the second section framed by repeat signs (first appearance in the set). Irregular phrase structure, with the same type of contrapuntal interplay as found in No. 23 although more elaborate. Introduction of the accent *sf*, used in this instance as a punctuating device at the ends of phrases.

No. 26. Repetition. (30") T2 M2
  Key center A; Mixolydian mode. Irregular phrase structure with repeated notes and slurs. Canonic imitation at the eleventh (fourth + octave). The principle of legato repeated notes found in No. 8 applies here.

No. 27. Syncopation. (35") T2 M2
(The exercise [Appendix, No. 3] for No. 27 deals with the figural difficulties and not with the principle of syncopation.)
  Key center C; major mode. Irregular phrase lengths, free counterpoint. The melody in the top voice is the same as in No. 9, but the present example has more rhythmic security since the suspension is always on the downbeat and under or over a played note in the other voice.

No. 28. Canon at the Octave. (30") T2 M2

Key center E; Phrygian mode. The same melody as in No. 8 but presented in canonic imitation at the octave. Can serve as an introductory piece to No. 29.

No. 29. Imitation Reflected. (30") T2 M2

(The exercise [Appendix, No. 4] for No. 29 presents a pentachord figure played in simultaneous inversion between the hands.)

Key center E; Mixolydian mode. Canonic imitation at the octave with the melody inverted in the lower voice. A good sight-reading piece, since the inversion is not a strict one.

No. 30. Canon at the Lower Fifth. Moderato. (43") T2 M2

Key center G; Mixolydian mode. Canonic imitation, actually at the fourth if one takes the interval literally. The canon in this case is strict, even at the final cadence. Playing the piece in parallel motion, voices beginning at the same time, might be a helpful preliminary exercise for coordination. The first piece in the set to use a tempo marking (all pieces in the *Mikrokosmos* have MM markings).

No. 31. Little Dance in Canon Form. Allegro. (35") T2 M2

Key center D; Dorian mode. Two sections, the second repeated. Strict canonic imitation at the octave. Another study in accents (>) continued from No. 21, but this time in alternation because of the canon. It is again advisable to do some preliminary practice in parallel motion.

No. 32. In Dorian Mode. Lento. (52") T3 M3

Key center D; Dorian mode. Free counterpoint. Although marked "p, legato" at the beginning, this is the first piece of the set in which phrase and slur indications are totally lacking. Note the Picardy third at the end, the first instance of one.

No. 33. Slow Dance. Andante. (45") T3 M3

Key center G; cadence on the dominant. Another example of free counterpoint with no phrase or slur marks. First instance of more than one dynamic in the same piece (introduction to terrace dynamics) and the "hairpin" crescendo. This and the previous example introduce for the first time compound meters (3/2 in No. 32 and 6/4 in No. 33), presenting side-by-side comparisons.

No. 34. In Phrygian Mode. Calmo. (45") T3 M3

Key center E; Phrygian mode. This, the darkest of the ecclesiastical modes, is said by Bartók to have been "used in Hungary for the last 150 years [as of 1945]."[8] Free counterpoint. Use of *sf*, dynamic changes, the first instance of "cresc." and "dim." indications. The feeling of crescendo is enhanced by a rhythmic hemiola in the top voice, and the diminuendo can be best achieved by carefully gauging the lower voice to the natural decay of the held B in the top voice.

No. 35. Chorale. Largamente. (1' 13") T4 M3

Key center C; major mode. Free counterpoint, quasi-canon style. Similarity to the chorale style of Bach in the four held-note cadences, which give focus to the harmonic structure (G/D, E, F, C). Angular interval relations make for tricky sight reading and coordination.

No. 36. Free Canon. Teneramente. (42") T3 M3

Key center A; Aeolian mode. Free counterpoint, quasi-canon style. Melodic emphasis on thirds and fourths; demands careful attention to melodic smoothness. This final example ends with the inscription "Péteré" (Bartók's son), to whom the first volume is dedicated.

Volume II: Nos. 37–66
T2–5 M2–5
21' 14"

No. 37. In Lydian Mode. Allegretto. (40") T3 M3

Key center F, cadence on dominant; Lydian mode. Strict canonic imitation at the octave. Introduction to the tenuto indication on repeated notes; these are always in conjunction with tied notes and are difficult to coordinate with them. Introduction to the fermata at the final cadence of this example.

No. 38. Staccato and Legato. Moderato. (15") T2 M2
(While the exercise [Appendix, No. 5] for No. 38 deals in a similar way with staccato-slur combinations, it is much different melodically and more difficult than the example it is supposed to preface. One could actually consider No. 38 a preparatory exercise for it.)

Key center D; major mode. Mirror setting of three-note legato slurs alternating with staccato repeated notes. Could also be a preparatory study for No. 39. Similar in style and difficulty to No. 5 of *The First Term at the Piano*, Sz. 53.

No. 39. Staccato and Legato. Comodo. (30") T3 M3

Key center F; major mode. Canonic setting of a variety of slur lengths alternating with staccato repeated notes. Difficult to coordinate because the touch schemes do not coincide as in the previous example. Remember that the touch is staccato, not staccatissimo (wedge), and the note can be shortened as much as one-half its value. Keep the melodic direction consistent in the repeated notes.

No. 40. In Yugoslav Mode. Allegretto. (1' 40") T3 M3

Key center E, cadence on dominant; Mixolydian mode. AABA form. Imitation of Yugoslavian bagpipe music, the lower voice representing the drone

and the upper voice the chanter. The word "mode" in the title does not refer
to Mixolydian, but to a style of music (the German *Art* is more precise) typi-
cally Yugoslavian. Introduction to the marcatissimo type of accent at the final
cadence. Similar in style and difficulty to No. 6 of *The First Term at the Piano*,
Sz 53.

No. 41. Melody with Accompaniment. Adagio. (40") T3 M4
(The exercises [Appendix, Nos. 6, 7, and 8] for Nos. 41 and 42 are preparatory
to the different types of accompaniment patterns found in these examples.)

Key center G; combination of Lydian (raised fourth) and Mixolydian
(lowered seventh) modes. Melody over barcarolle-type accompaniment. Note
the changes of direction in the accompaniment and the change of meter toward
the end. Demands sensitivity and a good ear for tonal balance.

No. 42. Accompaniment in Broken Triads. Andante tranquillo. (1' 20") T3
M4

Key center A; Aeolian mode. Two-phrase melody with broken-chord accompaniment, repeated with voices exchanged. The first piece in the set to use
a different dynamic (*p, mf*) for each voice. A good study in tonal balance,
especially in the second half, where the melody is in the lower voice; note the
hint of major in the accompaniment here. Marcatissimo with staccato is introduced for the first time.

Nos. 43 a and b. In Hungarian Style. Allegro. (30" each) T3 M2
(The exercise [Appendix, No. 9] for No. 43 treats the technical figure found in
the two versions, first in parallel motion, then in imitation.)

Key center D (a), G (b); Dorian mode. For two pianos. Etude in broken
thirds in Piano I accompanied by counterpoint in Piano II. The second version (b) presents the figure in quasi-imitation, resulting in some contrary-motion
playing. First instance of the indication "più forte."

No. 44. Contrary Motion. Vivace. (17") T3 M2

Key centers E and G-sharp; major modes. For two pianos. Two voices in
mirror figurations in Piano I accompanied by staccato counterpoint in Piano
II. Notice that the key signatures correspond only to the range of melodic activity on any given staff; this is merely a visual aid for reading and not an attempt to confuse the student. Bartók considers Piano II optional.[9]

No. 45. Méditation. Andante. (37") T4 M4

Key center F; Dorian mode. Melody with broken-chord accompaniment,
exchanged between the hands three times. This example is similar to No. 42
as a study in tonal balance with different dynamics for each voice. Coordination problems because of the changing contour of the accompaniment with each
appearance.

No. 46. Increasing—Diminishing. Moderato. (58") T4 M4

Key center E; Phrygian mode. A dynamic arch form, beginning *pp*, progressing to *f*, and diminishing back to *pp*. Bartók does not recommend this piece "for the average pupil."[10] A useful study in tonal control and gauging of dynamics. With the crescendo come interval expansion and faster note values; the reverse is true for the diminuendo. These factors can help achieve the dynamic effects through means other than touch.

No. 47. Big Fair. Vivace, con brio. (35") T5 M3

(The exercises [Appendix, Nos. 10 and 11] for No. 47 deal with broken fourths and pedal–hand coordination respectively. It is curious that Bartók reverted to the outmoded and often confusing scheme "𝄽 . . . ✳" and did not continue to use brackets as in earlier works.)

Key center A; Dorian mode, pentatonic scale figurations. Loose ABA form. The first pedal study of the set, used as a color device to help depict the busy and noisy atmosphere suggested by the title. Vigorous counterpoint in fourths and fifths relieved somewhat by stepwise activity at m. 14. Use of marcatissimo and sforzato accent types. Possibly the most difficult piece in this volume.

No. 48. In Mixolydian Mode. Allegro non troppo. (1') T4 M4

Key center G, cadence on dominant; Mixolydian mode. Through-composed melody with rolling accompaniment. Rotational technique needed in left hand; same angularity of melody as in No. 47, but in a more lyrical setting. Tests one's capacity for imaginative phrasing.

No. 49. Crescendo—Diminuendo. Moderato. (24") T5 M3

Key center C; major mode. Two-voice counterpoint. Fine study not only in dynamic gradations but also in slur-staccato combinations. A companion piece to No. 46, but technically more difficult.

No. 50. Minuetto. Tempo di Menuetto. (27") T3 M5

Key center A; Lydian and major modes. Two voices with inverted counterpoint in the first two phrases. Slur-staccato combinations. Has same grace and charm as similar examples by Bach and Mozart. Stylistically similar to No. 11 of *The First Term at the Piano*, Sz. 53.

No. 51. Waves. Andante. (1') T4 M4

Key center D-flat, cadence on dominant; pentatonic scale patterns. ABAB, the second half in inverted counterpoint. Study in black-key playing and legato execution of tied notes. The title suggests subtle dynamic effects not indicated in print; hands-separate or parallel-motion practice will help bring this about.

No. 52. Unison Divided. Allegro. (17") T3 M2

Key center G; Lydian, Mixolydian modes. Single melody (preferable to "unison," which implies more than one voice assuming the same pitch) divided

between the hands.   Demands tonal continuity and precise cutoffs when exchanging from one hand to the other.   A good preparatory exercise for similar
instances in the Bach sinfonias.

No. 53.   In Transylvanian Style.   Risoluto.   (36")   T4 M3
   Key center D; Dorian mode.   Single melody divided between the hands giving
way to two-voice counterpoint.   Both voices in bass clef for the first eight
measures, in treble clef for the rest of the piece—a new sight-reading challenge.
Transylvania was part of Hungary until 1920, when it was annexed to Romania.
Typical of the folk style in that region is the two eighth notes and a quarter note
rhythm that permeates this example.

No. 54.   Chromatic.   Andante.   (15")   T4 M3
   Key center E; chromatic scale figurations negate any feeling of mode.   Two
voices in unison and counterpoint.   A large hand will have trouble with this example if one adheres to the five-finger position (Bartók's obvious intention, judg-
ing by the initial fingerings) rather than the conventional chromatic scale
fingering.

No. 55.   Triplets on Lydian Mode.   Tempo di marcia.   (30")   T4 M4
(The exercises [Appendix, Nos. 12 and 13] for No. 55 deal with the rhythmic
challenge of duplet vs. triplet and parallel fifths respectively.)
   Key center F; Lydian mode.   For two pianos.   Melody in duplets and triplets
accompanied by repeated fifths in Piano I (the first instance in the set of writing in more than two voices), imitation in octaves in Piano II.   This example
presents some of the most effective ways to deal with this rhythmic problem: a
strong metric pulse in the accompaniment, and the use of a second piano
(preferably by the teacher) providing rhythmic security and reinforcement.

No. 56.   Melody in Tenths.   Risoluto.   (15")   T3 M3
(The exercise [Appendix, No. 14] for No. 56 is a good introductory drill for
held against moving voices in the same hand.)
   Key center A; Dorian mode.   Four-voice counterpoint.   Four phrases, each
presenting a different arrangement of held against moving voices.   Good introductory material for the Bach sinfonias.

No. 57.   Accents.   Non troppo vivo.   (47")   T5 M3
   Key center A; combined modes, modulatory.   Two-voice canon, mostly at
the octave, going through four changes of key signature.   Excellent sight-reading
material for both finger coordination and key recognition.   Two different types
of accents on different pulses.

No. 58.   In Oriental Style.   Assai lento.   (55")   T4 M4
   Key center G; non-diatonic mode based on Arabic scale (augmented second
between third and fourth scale degrees).   Two-voice canon at the octave.   This

example reflects Bartók's folk-music excursions in North Africa in 1913. A stretching exercise for fingers 2 and 3 of the left hand, and 3 and 4 of the right hand. Dynamic arch form (*p–mf–p*).

No. 59. Major and Minor. Lento. (42") T3 M4

Key center F; Lydian and Aeolian modes. Free counterpoint in two voices, the two modes superimposed and exchanged twice. Three types of accent. No change of five-finger positions, but accidentals are variable.

No. 60. Canon with Sustained Notes. Grave. (42") T3 M4

Key center E; major mode. Four-voice canon at the fourth and fifth. An extension of the principle of No. 56, that of sustaining tied notes with moving voices in the same hand. The separating signs (|) indicating phrase endings occur at different times in each hand because of the canon, and must be vigilantly observed. Meters of 2/2 and 1/2.

No. 61. Pentatonic Melody. Moderato. (50") T5 M4

Key center C; Lydian mode (melody in A Aeolian). Binary form, melody over ostinato accompaniment, voices reversed in second section. The pentatonic scale presents the most prevalent form of folk melody and is used worldwide in many different forms. Good exercise in tonal balance of melody over accompaniment, especially when the melody appears "in rilievo" in the left hand.

No. 62. Minor Sixths in Parallel Motion. Vivace, ma non troppo, risoluto. (40") T3 M4
(The exercise [Appendix, No. 16] for No. 62 is basically a drill for white-to-black key movement in fingers 3 and 4 in the right hand, and 4 and 5 in the left.)

Key center A; bitonal. Two voices in parallel motion, almost consistently a minor sixth apart. Aside from the technical benefits, this example is good ear training for recognizing the minor sixth, which is often confused with the major sixth because of context.

No. 63. Buzzing. Con moto. (37") T4 M4

Key center B; Locrian mode. Melody over trill-like ostinato, voices exchanged midway. Bartók frequently exploited the semitone to provide an aural effect suggestive of the buzzing of insects (see also Vol. IV, No. 142 of this series, and "Musiques Nocturnes" from *Out of Doors*, Sz. 81). The execution of the present example is made particularly difficult by Bartók's initial fingerings (black-to-white key movements of fingers 5 and 4 in the left hand, and 1 and 2 in the right).

Nos. 64a and b. Line and Point. Allegro. (30" each) T3 M4

Key centers G and E; Aeolian modes (a). Key center C; chromatic (b). Four-voice counterpoint using the same fan-out technique of sustained voice

against moving voice as in No. 60. The main difference between the two seg-
ments of this example is obvious: diatonic scale movement (a) and chromatic
scale movement (b), the latter representing a folk-music practice that Bartók
discovered in the Dalmatian area of Yugoslavia. These chromatic melodies are
"nothing else than diatonic melodies of the neighbouring areas, compressed into
a chromatic level."[11]

No. 65. Dialogue. Allegretto. (37") T4 M3
(The exercises [Appendix, Nos. 17a and b] for No. 65 deal with staccato parallel fifths in every type of black–white key configuration.)

Key center D; Dorian mode (Bartók says "D minor with altered sixth,"[12]
but the melody lacks a B-flat). The same folk melody as in Vol. I, No. 14, of
this series, but presented with vocal text in a melody–accompaniment setting.
In the Notes at the end of this volume, Bartók suggests ways that this piece can
be presented on one or two pianos. The parallel fifths are best played with a
light wrist staccato.

No. 66. Melody Divided. Andante. (1' 8") T4 M4
(The exercises [Appendix, Nos. 18a, b, c, and d] for No. 66 provide drill for
interval contraction, mainly fifths [fingers 5 and 1] to thirds [4 and 2] to single
note [3]. Some of the exercises are actually more difficult than the examples
they are supposed to preface.)

Key center E; pentatonic melody. Four phrases of melody against double-
note accompaniment, with exchange of voices with each phrase, and short coda.
The main difficulty is not the double-note accompaniment but the tonal balance
of melody over and, especially, under accompaniment. As indicated by the inscription at the end of this example, "Péteré," this volume, along with Vol. I,
is dedicated to Bartók's son Peter.

Volume III: Nos. 67–96
T3-8 M3-7
25' 19"

No. 67. Thirds against a Single Voice. Andante. (35") T3 M4
(The exercises [Appendix, Nos. 19 and 20] for No. 67 present the coordination
problem of held note against two voices in parallel thirds.)

Key center A; Aeolian mode. Three-voice textures of the type of melodic
movement indicated in the title. Difficulties consist of maintaining full value
on the tied notes, gauging a long-range crescendo of five measures, and simul-
taneity of thirds. Tonal balance might be a factor to be introduced here.

No. 68. Hungarian Dance. Allegro con spirito. (30") T5 M4
Key center D; major mode. For two pianos. New Style folk melody with
broken-chord accompaniment. Piano can be played alone. Note the subtle

melodic inflections in the accompaniment in Piano I. Symmetrical inversion (Piano I) in last three measures.

No. 69. Chord Study. Moderato. (1') T5 M4
(The exercises [Appendix, Nos. 21a and b] for No. 69 contain the same parallel triad patterns used in the example but they are played simultaneously and in mirror fashion for greater security.)

Key center G. Melody over parallel staccato triads, parts exchanged midway. A continuation of the technical situation in No. 65 (parallel fifths) and a good study in hand position and wrist staccato. The need for expressive cantabile in the melodic portions should not be overlooked. First appearance of the indication "simile" (mm. 5 and 22). Give careful attention to durations in the chord parts. Transcribed for two pianos in Sz. 108.

No. 70. Melody against Double Notes. Adagio. (1' 8") T4 M4
Key center D (fundamental); F-sharp Mixolydian in upper voice. Melody with two-voice accompaniment, parts exchanged midway. A continuation of the technical situation in No. 66 (fifths diminishing to thirds). The dual key signatures create a bitonal appearance, but the final cadence is clearly D major. First appearance of the indications "sopra" (above) and "sotto" (below) for positioning of the hands.

No. 71. Thirds. Grave. (1' 15") T4 M4
Key center D; Aeolian mode with cadences in major. Four-voice counterpoint, parallel thirds in each hand. A continuation of the technical situation in No. 67, and the exercises for it (Appendix, Nos. 19 and 20) can be used here also. Meter and tempo changes, the latter introduced for the first time.

No. 72. Dragon's Dance. Molto pesante. (30") T3 M3
Key center G; Lydian mode. Held notes against slurs and staccato in each hand. The grotesque characterization suggested in the title is provided by the emphasis on the tritone. Although the tempo indication asks for a heavy touch, be sure to save tone for the marcatissimos that occur at cadences. For the first time in this series, almost midway through, we find hand extension beyond the five-finger position. Similar in content and difficulty to No. 12 of *The First Term at the Piano*, Sz. 53.

No. 73. Sixths and Triads. Comodo. (37") T5 M3
(The exercises for No. 73 present pedal drills [Appendix, No. 22] and first- and second-inversion triads in parallel motion using diatonic and chromatic scale patterns [Appendix, Nos. 23a, b, c, and d]. The example itself makes no use of the pedal.)

Key center G; Mixolydian mode. Sixths in quasi-imitation and first- and second-inversion triads in parallel diatonic motion. An expanded version of No.

69, requiring the same kind of touch. Introduction to the indication "subito f." Similar in content and difficulty to No. 11 of *The First Term at the Piano*, Sz. 53.

Nos. 74a and b. Hungarian Song. Allegro moderato. (38" each) T6 M4

> Erzsi, bring my hat, that no maiden can look into my shining eyes. [Mixed Style melody. Translation in B&H is not a literal one, but is altered to fit a poetic scheme in English. Same tune used in No 10. of *The First Term at the Piano*, Sz. 53.]

Key center C; Aeolian mode. Three variations with interlude material. First version (a), for piano solo, has balance and coordination difficulties. Second verions (b) can be performed by voice and piano, by another instrument and piano, or as a piano duet.

No. 75. Triplets. Andante. (54") T5 M4

Key center C; Lydian mode (cadence in D major). A continuation of the rhythmic principle of triplet vs. duplet in No. 55, but this time with a legato rather than a punctuated accompaniment. Shifting meters. A solid preconceived feeling of quarter-note pulse should be felt.

No. 76. In Three Parts. Allegro molto. (27") T6 M4

(The exercise [Appendix, No. 24] emphasizes held vs. staccato moving voices.)

Key center D; Mixolydian and Lydian modes. Three-voice counterpoint of held vs. legato and staccatissimo moving voices. More difficult than it appears on the page: the coordination of the three different touches along with occasional marcatissimos is a formidable task.

No. 77. Little Study. Allegro risoluto. (36") T5 M4

(The exercise [Appendix, No. 24] was most likely meant for No. 76 because of its emphasis on held vs. staccato moving voices. The exercises for No. 77 [Appendix, Nos. 25a and b] deal with similar figural patterns.)

Key center G; Dorian mode, some cadences in major. Two voices in parallel motion except at cadences. An etude for both hands involved with figurations covering the interval of the sixth. A stretch of a third between fingers 4 and 5 of the left hand. It might be helpful to practice the voices in mirror formation for more technical security of each hand and equal technical benefit of both.

No. 78. Five-tone Scale. Allegro. (27") T4 M5

Key center E; Aeolian mode, pentatonic scale patterns. Two voices in counterpoint, both using the principle of pentatony (five-note scale, no half-steps). A good study in coordination of different-size phrasings and slurrings. Sensitivity and musical finesse called for.

No. 79. Hommage à J. S. B. (50") T6 M5

(The exercises [Appendix, Nos. 26a, b, and d; 27a and b; and 28] for No. 79

offer a number of technical figurations found in the example and introduce a
new dimension to the *Mikrokosmos*, that of basic five-finger drill of the type found
in Bach, Clementi, and Czerny.)

Key center E; major mode (the key signature indicates E minor). Two-voice
counterpoint. The same triadic and figural counterpoint as in many of the
preludes of J. S. Bach. Different finger combinations are exercised within the
span of the perfect and diminished fifth; some chromatics. The penultimate
measure is a rhythmic "tongue twister" for the fingers.

No. 80. Hommage à R. Sch. (37") T5 M5

Key center C; Aeolian mode with frequent accidental changes. Two voices
in counterpoint, dotted rhythms against even eighth notes; two sections, one an
inversion of the other. The most obvious links between this example and the
style of Robert Schumann are chromatic harmonic effects and rhythmic interest. The legato indication in one voice and the lack thereof in the other implies
a slight difference in articulation.

No. 81. Wandering. Non troppo lento. (1') T5 M5

Key center G; modulatory. Two voices in counterpoint; imitation and inversion. A wide variety of five-finger configurations, providing good pentachord exercises. Dynamics range from *pp* to *mp*, but change frequently.
Coordination difficulties of different size phrasings.

No. 82. Scherzo. Allegretto scherzando. (30") T5 M4
(The exercises [Appendix, Nos. 29 a, b, and c] for No. 82 are basically rhythmic in nature, introducing the 7/8 rhythm that is found in the example.)

Key center D; Lydian mode. Four-voice texture of seconds, thirds, and
fourths in syncopation. Introduces 7/8 meter (can be subdivided 4/8 + 3/8 for
better recognition); frequent metric changes. Marcato and marcatissimo indications. Coincident slurrings, but of different lengths. Demands rhythmic
precision and vitality.

No. 83. Melody with Interruptions. Risoluto e pesante. (45") T5 M5

"Hungarian folk tune: genuine, not made up [translation unavailable]."[13]

Key center G; Mixolydian mode. Alternation of double-note figuration and
folk tune. Good exercise in shifting registers and textures. The pedal indications are designed to sustain the last chords of the double-note figurations, the
eighth rests indicating lifts rather than silences (this can be explained as similar
to the pedal–rest discrepancies found in much nineteenth-century piano music).
An elaboration of the technical principle in No. 66.

No. 84. Merriment. Vivace. (45") T5 M5

Key center E; Mixolydian mode. Alternation of syncopated material with pentatonic melody, similar to No. 3 of *Three Rondos*, Sz. 84. Requires smooth-ness in transferring melody from one hand to the other; pay particular atten-tion to the double stems. Coordination difficulties of non-coincident phrase lengths, mm. 18 and 19.

No. 85. Broken Chords. Andante. (1' 17") T6 M6
(The exercises [Appendix, Nos. 30a and b and 31] for No. 85 deal mainly with the section in which broken seventh chords predominate. They are presented in the form of blocked and arpeggiated chords. No. 31 presents the seventh chord resolving to the triad.)

Key center G; Mixolydian mode. One- and two-voice textures in broken triad and seventh-chord formation. A continuation of the difficulties presented in No. 84, where legato and smoothness of transfer are called for, without break or overlap. Long-range dynamic arch form extends throughout most of the piece (*p–mf–p; f* introduction and coda).

No. 86. Two Major Pentachords. Andante. (1' 18") T5 M5
Key centers F-sharp (bass clef) and C (treble clef); major mode. Bitonal counterpoint exploiting a wide variety of scale and triadic formations. Consis-tent five-finger positions throughout. Study in smooth legato and finger coor-dination between the hands. A long-range crescendo over almost nine measures.

No. 87. Variations. Allegro moderato. (1' 20") T5 M6
Key center D; Dorian mode with hint of Mixolydian in accompaniment and variation 2. Melody, similar in structure to a Hungarian folk tune, with two variations, each having a tempo, character, or meter change. Much dialogue between hands. Melodies are natural and uncontrived, resulting in a splendid study in lyrical and expressive playing.

No. 88. Duet for Pipes. Molto moderato. (1') T5 M5
Key center D. Two-voice counterpoint, probably in imitation of primitive or exotic instruments. Wandering melodies result in indeterminate tonalities. Triplet and duplet rhythms juxtaposed, not yet superimposed; a continuation of the rhythmic features of Nos. 75 and 55. Legato phrasings of different lengths throughout with the exception of m. 5.

No. 89. In Four Parts. Largo. (53") T5 M6
Key center A; Mixolydian mode. Four voices in free counterpoint. Good introduction to the complexities of non-simultaneous melodic movement in Bach counterpoint. Examples of diminution and inversion at mm. 9–13.

No. 90. In Russian Style. Pesante. (37") T6 M5

"Not an original Russian tune, but in the style: short themes and sentences, repeti-tion."[14]

Key center C; mixed scale patterns. Folk-type melody exchanged between hands accompanied by slurred accompaniments (bagpipe?). Slurs of different lengths pose a coordination challenge. Intervals of many kinds, especially augmented and diminished ones.

No. 91. Chromatic Invention (1). Lento. (55") T6 M6

Key center E. Canon at the octave and the ninth and in inversion; varying distances between points of imitation. A twentieth-century analogue of the Bach invention. Influence of Arabic music likely, because of chromatics and augmented seconds.

No. 92. Chromatic Invention (2). Allegro robusto. (40") T8 M5

Key center E; chromatic and tritonal movement. Two-voice counterpoint in parallel, imitative, and free melodic patterns; trill ostinato in left hand throughout most of second half, which contains frequent crossovers of right hand. Expanded range of the keyboard. Although only in two voices, this example offers unusually severe coordination problems, which surpass those of many of the Bach inventions.

No. 93. In Four Parts. Molto moderato, sonoro. (37") T6 M6

Key center G; major and Mixolydian modes. A four-voice invention, continuing the principle of No. 89, that of a preparation for Bach counterpoint. Held vs. moving voices, meter changes (one in 5/8), and the separating sign (|) at unexpected places present the main challenges.

No. 94. Tale. Moderato. (55") T5 M7

Key center C; Aeolian mode. Imitative counterpoint in two and three voices at different intervals; points of imitation from one to five measures. Constantly shifting registers and meters. Narrative quality (the translation from the German and Hungarian is "Once upon a time"). Note the comma separation between mm. 10 and 11.

Nos. 95 a and b. Song of the Fox. Allegro con brio. (40" each) T5 M7

The priest has no breeches, only a cassock [Hungarian folk tune].

Key center D; Ionian mode. First version (a) set for solo piano, second (b) for voice and piano accompaniment with opportunity for the ensembles described in Nos. 65 and 74. Use of the inverted dotted rhythm. Requires wit and imagination; study, recite, and sing the text (in B&H) for the proper spirit.

No. 96. Stumblings. Allegretto. (45") T5 M6

Key center G; Aeolian and Mixolydian modes. Two voices in parallel and contrary motion. The example is in 3/4, and the main difficulty is avoiding the metric appearance of 6/8, which is often suggested by the melodic patterns and changes of fingering patterns.

Volume IV: Nos. 97–121
T5–10 M4–8
27' 5"

No. 97. Notturno. Adagio. (1' 40") T5 M7

Key center E; Aeolian mode. Melody over rolling triadic accompaniment, voices exchanged toward the end. A fine prototype of the nineteenth-century nocturne in the best traditions of Chopin and Field, but without the ornamental filigree. A good study in thumb independence and rotational motion for the left hand. The best way to achieve the cantabile effect is to think through rests and to avoid abrupt cutoffs, even where staccato is indicated. Observe precise pedal indications, noting that the "(sim.)" indications continue the pedal duration immediately preceding.

No. 98. Thumb Under. Allegro non troppo. (1') T5 M4
(The exercise [Appendix, No. 32] for No. 98 introduces a new dimension in the *Mikrokosmos*, namely, the scale position rather than the five-finger position of most previous examples. The two hands receive equal benefit of the scale exercise.)

Key center G; Dorian mode with raised fourth. Two voices basically in parallel motion at the octave. The most difficult aspect of this example is that the thumbs sometimes play simultaneously, sometimes not. Fingerings should be carefully observed, even though they do not always seem the most practical.

No. 99. Crossed Hands. Lento. (1') T6 M5

Key center C; non-diatonic modes. Different scale patterns resulting in diminished-chord outlines; different key signatures in each voice. Frequently crossed hands cause coordination difficulties; a great sight-reading challenge.

No. 100. In the style of a Folk Song. Andante. (45") T6 M7

"A Balkan melody, not my own invention [translation unavailable]."[15]

Key center A; Dorian, mixed modes. Melody over one-voice counterpoint, voices exchanged midway. Long phrases of varying lengths. Shifting meters, alternating between 5/8 and 3/8. Excellent study in legato.

No. 101. Diminished Fifth. Con moto. (57") T5 M6

Key centers E, A-flat. Two voices in counterpoint, shifting tetrachord formations a tritone apart. Good sight-reading example emphasizing shifting hand positions. Example of rhythmic augmentation in mm. 33–34.

No. 102. Harmonics. Allegro non troppo, un poco rubato. (1' 21") T8 M7

Key center B; Mixolydian mode. Melody interrupted by accented triads sustained by the sympathetic vibrations of silently depressed chords. The technique of harmonics, or overtones, is widely used among twentieth-century composers, but this is Bartók's only use of it in his piano music. A difficult piece, mainly because of the widely spaced chordal jumps in the right hand and the need to depress chords silently on a metric pulse (possibly explaining the "un poco rubato" indication). The "sim." indication at m. 36 obviously refers to the 5-3-1 fingering for the triads. Two types of staccatos (wedge and dot), sharp accents, and frequent tempo changes all keep the performer busy.

No. 103. Minor and Major. Molto allegro. (1' 15") T8 M7

Key center E at cadence; result of convergence of A minor and B major (bitonal effect). ABA form. Complex rhythm, with irregular subdivisions of 9/8, 8/8, 7/8, 5/8, and 3 x 2/8 meters. A rudimentary example of rhythmic structures found in Bulgarian dance music, examples of which occur subsequently in this series. Ten-measure accelerando at end; the performer is given the latitude of repeating the figure as many times as needed to arrive at the "presto" tempo ("rep. ad libitum," an indication found in No. 2 of *Elegies*, Sz. 41, and No. 3 of *Out of Doors*, Sz. 81).

Nos. 104 a and b. Through the Keys. Comodo. (30" each) T6 M6

Key center D; variable modes. Two voices in parallel motion an octave apart (part a) and a tenth apart (part b), progressing through D major, A major, E major, C Phrygian, G Aeolian, and D Mixolydian. The basic technical principle of No. 98, that of thumb crossings in scale passages, is equally applicable here (Appendix, No. 32 would also be a useful exercise for this example).

No. 105. Playsong. Allegro. (1') T7 M6

Key centers C-sharp (lower voice) and D (upper voice); pentatonic scale patterns. Two to four voices in imitative, mirror, and free counterpoint. Interval of a third between fingers 2 and 3 in both hands. Two basic components, one lyrical, one "con brio, marcato." Exotic harmonic effects from the combination of the two tonalities.

No. 106. Children's Song. Moderato. (1' 5") T7 M6

Key center F-sharp; bitonal scale patterns. Two and three voices in imitative and free counterpoint. A sequel to No. 105 in the presentation of bitonal effects. Frequent tempo changes. Difficulties of held vs. moving voices in the left hand.

No. 107. Melody in the Mist. Tranquillo. (1' 10") T6 M8

Key center G; pentatonic chord and scale patterns. A mysterious mood created by the alternation of cluster-type chords and unison melody; compare similar instances in the fourth movement of *Dance Suite*, Sz. 77, and the second movement of *Concerto No. 2*, Sz. 95. Introduces color effects found in the piano music of Debussy and Ravel. Pedal markings should be strictly observed for proper effect.

No. 108. Wrestling. Allegro non troppo. (1') T8 M6

Key center D; alternation between major and minor. A series of sustained tones encompassed by moving voices in each hand. This is an example of musical gesture, in which the stressful and sometimes painful act of wrestling is portrayed. Although it would be tempting to use the sostenuto pedal to sustain the long tones, the whole effect of the obvious pianistic "struggle" would be lost by this simplification (this advice also applies to the first movement, mm. 140–166, of the *Sonata*, Sz. 80).

No. 109. From the Island of Bali. Andante. (1' 56") T7 M8

Key centers D and F; minor modes. Two voices in imitative, mirror, parallel, and free melodic patterns. Tritonal harmonic effects prevail throughout. ABA form with contrasting moods ("dolce" and "risoluto"). The alluring and then festive atmosphere of a tropical island is portrayed. The term "Prol. Ped.," indicated for the final fourteen measures, means that the pedal D's can be sustained with the sostenuto (middle) pedal, if available, or with a very careful use of the damper pedal; it is also possible, even preferable, to use the two in combination.

No. 110. Clashing Sounds. Assai allegro. (1' 8") T7 M6

Key center E (F-flat); chromatic scale patterns. Fifths and thirds a half-step apart for dissonant effect, alternating with a sustained section at a slower tempo. ABABA form. Pay particular attention to the indication "mezza voce" at each statement of A to avoid too harsh a sound; let the dissonance and rhythmic drive provide the excitement while maintaining a light but slightly accented touch. The indication "1/2 pedal" means to hold the pedal halfway down, resting at the point of resistance; this will create a slight echo while maintaining the marcato effects.

No. 111. Intermezzo. Molto tranquillo. (1' 38") T6 M7

"Characteristic Hungarian style. . . ."[16]

Key center D-sharp. Three voices in imitative, inverted, and free counterpoint. The phrase structure of a Hungarian folk tune (AABBA) is presented in the style of a three-part invention, with much melodic development of the main theme. Melancholy, meditative mood.

No. 112. Variations on a Folk Tune. Allegro, ben ritmato. (1') T7 M6

"Original (well-known) Hungarian song. . . ."[17] [The tune is similar to that of No. 8 of *Ten Easy Pieces*, Sz. 39.]

I would like to plow, to drive six oxen, provided my love would come to hold the plow.

Key center D; Ionian mode. Four variations using parallel octaves, parallel sixths in imitation, and chromatic imitation. The parallel sixth is the main technical feature, a continuation of that of No. 73. The fingering indications "1 + 2" (combination of fingers 1 and 2 for each tone) can actually be substituted for 3 reinforced by 1 and 2.

No. 113. Bulgarian Rhythm (1). Allegro molto. (1') T8 (T10 with octave doublings) M6

"The theme is Hungarian and the rhythm is Bulgarian."[18]

Key center D; Dorian mode. Four-phrase melody framed by introduction and coda, both emphasizing the dominant. Bartók advises that the repetition can be played with octave doublings (see his Notes). This is one of two examples in this volume of Bulgarian rhythm, a folk style that is fully realized in "Six Dances in Bulgarian Rhythm," Nos. 148–153 of this series (see especially No. 149). The meter here is 7/8, but it could have been notated 2 + 2 + 3 because of the rhythmic subdivisions.

No. 114. Theme and Inversion. Molto moderato. (1' 15") T7 M7

Key center B; Aeolian mode. Introduction, interlude, and coda alternating with a melody with contrapuntal accompaniment. The melody is in the top voice at first appearance, then in the lower voice in inversion, in an example of inverted counterpoint found in the Bach inventions.

No. 115. Bulgarian Rhythm (2). Vivace. (23") T8 M7

"This is an original Bulgarian theme."[19]

Key center G; scale patterns altered chromatically. Melody with contrapuntal and then chordal accompaniment. This example is a protoytpe of No. 150 because of its subdivided 5/8 meter and similar melodic and phrase structure. Note the mirror writing at mm. 20–21.

No. 116. Melody. Tempo di Marcia. (1' 30") T6 M7

Key center G; scale patterns altered chromatically. Structure composed of variational treatment (parallel motion, imitation, melody and accompaniment in the main themes). Examples of the inverted dotted rhythm found in much Hungarian folk music, as well as the ABCD phrase structure of the Old Style. Requires balance of left hand over right in the outer statements and sensitivity to different-size phrase structures.

No. 117. Bourée. Allegretto. (1') T6 M8

Key center D; mixed modes. Two-voice counterpoint with sustained tones providing a third and fourth voice. Free variation form on the motive found in the upper voice of m. 1. A twentieth-century prototype of the Baroque dance indicated in the title. Introduction to the "subito piano" change of dynamic and to crossed hands.

No. 118. Triplets in 9/8 Time. Allegro. (57") T6 M7

Key center C; mixed modes. Two-voice counterpoint in parallel motion and imitation at different intervals. Difficulties in counting, especially during sustained tones and rests.

No. 119. Dance in 3/4 Time. Allegretto grazioso. (50") T6 M8

Key center E; mixed modes. Two voices in free counterpoint. An experimental piece that may not appeal to the average student. Needs the rhythmic grace and lilt of a Baroque minuet.

No. 120. Fifth Chords. Allegro. (1') T7 M6

Key center C; mixed modes. Root-position triads in parallel motion in dialogue fashion between the hands in a variety of configurations. Frequent changes of meter. Long-range accelerandos extending through most of the piece, increasing the tempo from quarter note = 160 at the beginning to half note = 108 at m. 31. Tenuto and staccato touches. Although rebound facility in the triads is needed in this example, more difficult instances of the same technique are found in No. 102.

No. 121. Two-Part Study. Moderato. (1' 15") T7 M7

Key center D; Lydian mode. Two voices in mirror counterpoint and imitation. In m. 1, the held notes are not slurred to those in the following measure, but are sustained slightly into the measure to give a momentary chordal effect. Occasional separating signs (|) suggest more of a break than phrase separations.

Volume V: Nos. 122–139
T6–10+ M4–9
17' 46"

No. 122. Chords Together and Opposed. Molto vivace. (55") T9 M7

Key center G. Triadic formations in both hands with the moving voices generally in the middle. Theme with three variations. A good study in tonal balance and for strengthening fingers 2, 3, and 4. The last thirteen measures use the quasi-cluster technique found in some of Bartók's 1926 piano pieces (*Sonata*, Sz. 80, and "With Drums and Pipes" from *Out of Doors*, Sz. 81).

Nos. 123a and b. Staccato and Legato. Allegro. (50") T8 M7

Key center C. Two voices in strict canon at the fourth (part a) and fifth (part b); inverted counterpoint in part b. A difficult piece to coordinate because of the varying phrase lengths and non-simultaneous staccato and legato between the hands. Section b is more difficult because of its varied dynamic scheme. Much rhythmic syncopation but no metric changes.

No. 124. Staccato. Allegretto mosso. (1' 8") T7 M6

Key center A. Two voices exchanging repeated-note ostinatos and staccato melodies. Rhythmic syncopations. The MM marking is slow enough to accommodate both finger and wrist staccato; both types can be introduced here and used in different combinations.

No. 125. Boating. Allegretto. (1' 20") T7 M8

Key center G; pentatonic scale patterns on the black keys. Two voices exchanging melody and accompaniment, the latter in 3/4 meter with a melodic pattern suggestive of 6/8. A good introductory piece to "Barcarolla" from *Out of Doors*, requiring the same control of finger legato in both voices and adjustment to changes in meter.

No. 126. Change of Time. Allegro pesante. (40") T8 M7

Key center C; Mixolydian mode. Chordal setting of a Romanian-style folk tune presented in a repeated metric pattern of 2/4, 3/4, 3/8, and 5/8. Since the prescribed MM marking of eighth note = 250 cannot be used on most metronomes, the setting quarter note = 126 can be used despite the changes of meter.

No. 127. New Hungarian Folk Song. Ben ritmato. (55") T6 M8

> I would make a good star, because I would always glitter in the sky; about midnight I would go across the sky, to find my dear lover.

Key center B; Aeolian mode (piano cadence in D major), pentatonic melody. Two-verse melody with piano accompaniment in repeated chords followed by counterpoint. See Bartók's remarks in the Notes for different ways this piece can be performed. Provides an opportunity for accompaniment experience similar to that of No. 74.

No. 128. Peasant Dance. Moderato. (1' 13") T7 M8

> "An original [Bartók] theme but in old Hungarian modal style."[20]

Key center G; mixed modes. Four-phrase melody subject to motivic development ("Un poco più mosso") and ornamental embroidery ("Meno mosso"). A fine example of the way a melody can be developed in a variation form. Changing moods, tempi, and meters.

No. 129. Alternating Thirds. Allegro molto. (47") T9 M6

Key center E. Built exclusively on the interval of the third, mostly on the white keys. Uses only fingers 2 and 4 in each hand. A good introduction to Debussy's "Les tierces alternées" (*Préludes*, Vol. II), in which the same technical principle is used. Maintain a close weighty portato approach to the keys to avoid any superficial "slapping."

No. 130. Village Joke. Moderato. (45") T7 M8

Key center C; Lydian mode. Theme with melodic variation. Melody with syncopated accompaniment figures primarily designed to enhance the humorous effect. Coordination problem of turn figures in quintuplets against offbeat eighth notes.

No. 131. Fourths. Allegro non troppo. (45") T8 M7

Key centers E-flat, G-flat. Four-part mirror patterns built exclusively on the interval of the fourth provide an introduction to quartal harmony and bitonality. Awkward finger combinations and varied syncopations.

No. 132. Major Seconds Broken and Together. Adagio. (1' 30") T7 M9

Key center B; chromatic scale patterns. Alternating melody with accompaniment in sustained whole tones; many chromatic scale formations. The fingerings are designed to assure a smooth legato without aid of the pedal. A good companion piece to No. 144, which also emphasizes the interval of the minor second.

No. 133. Syncopation. Allegro. (1' 5") T10 M7

Key center G. Triads and slurs presented in syncopated rhythms with metric changes. A continuation of the rhythmic difficulties of the last fifteen measures of No. 126. Although Bartók cites this example as a "Good preparation for Prokofiev,"[21] it seems to be a more suitable introduction to the rhythmic complexities in some of Bartók's own piano works of 1926.

No. 134. Studies in Double Notes. Allegro. T10+ M4

These preparatory exercises to No. 135 are similar to those found in the appendixes in previous volumes, but here they are presented as a separate piece. The main emphasis is on thirds (fingers 1 and 5) and seconds (fingers 2 and 3) presented in parallel motion (No. 1), mirror formation (No. 2), and parallel motion covering more than three octaves (No. 3). These studies are similar to some of the stretching exercises of Pischna and should be approached with caution.

No. 135. Perpetuum Mobile. Allegro molto. (30") T10+ M6

Key center F. Eighth-note motion throughout featuring the same technical difficulty as in the previous example. Some melodic and figural similarities to the Schumann *Toccata*, Op. 7. A fingering of 2 and 4 in both hands could be used on the augmented seconds. The inscription "repet. ad infinitum" obviously refers to the repetition of the two closing chords for more of a climactic effect. As with No. 134, proceed with caution.

No. 136. Whole-tone Scale. Andante. (1' 35") T8 M7

Key center A. Whole-tone melodies in parallel motion and imitation with sustained tones. Free variation form. A variety of interesting harmonic effects are produced by the combination of similar (m. 7) and different (m. 13) whole-tone scales. Frequent hand position indications ("sopra," "sotto") require vigilant choreography.

No. 137. Unison. Moderato. (1' 40") T7 M7

Key center F-sharp; Phrygian mode. Built exclusively on parallel motion in octaves with frequent changes in hand position. A good sight-reading example to help develop spatial awareness at the keyboard and to adjust to frequent metric changes.

No. 138. Bagpipe. Allegretto. (1' 10") T11 M8

Key center G; mixed modes. Three-voice texture to exemplify the different components of the bagpipe: "chanter [top], tonic and dominant [middle], and the drone [bottom]." Bartók also mentions the typical "squeaky effects" of the instrument (beginning in m. 34) and "the air . . . going out of the pipes" (beginning with the diminuendo, m. 64).[22] A very difficult piece to memorize because of its random melodic patterns. The quintuplet trill figure against the duplet at m. 8 poses the same rhythmic problem as No. 130. Some tricky technical situations involving fingers 1 (e.g., m. 15) and 5 (last two measures).

No. 139. Merry Andrew. Con moto, scherzando. (58") T8 M8

Key center F. Triadic melody with varied accompaniment patterns exchanged between the voices. A musical portrayal of a buffoon or clown. An appealing piece with no technical difficulties other than hands occasionally in close position (at m. 7, keep the left hand under) and descending slur figures. A companion piece to No. 130.

Volume VI: Nos. 140–153
T8–12 M9–13
24' 59"

No. 140. Free Variations. Allegro molto. (1' 40") T11 M10

Key center A. Theme with four variations. A good study in coordinating repeated notes in the thumb with moving voices in the other fingers. Frequent metric changes and accents of every kind.

No. 141. Subject and Reflection. Allegro. (1' 16") T8 M9

Key center B-flat. Pure rondo form: ABACDA and coda, progressing through a systematic key pattern: B-flat, B, D, E-flat, F-sharp, G, B-flat. Four-voice textures mostly in mirror formation, five-finger position. The tonic in each key change is in the middle (thumbs) rather than in the bass. Sudden dynamic and tempo changes. Excellent study in counterpoint.

No. 142. From the Diary of a Fly. Allegro. (1' 35") T12 M9

Key center G. One of the finest examples of the character piece as used by

Bartók. Buzzing sounds of an insect are depicted by semitonal effects produced by the convergence of the two types of whole-tone scale. Bartók describes the climactic section ("Agitato," m. 49) as "the desperate sound of a fly's buzz, when getting into a cob-web" and subsequently ("con gioia, leggero," m. 59) when "he escapes."[23] He also suggests the use of a light, close-to-keys wrist staccato. Frequent adjustments in hand position ("sopra," "sotto"), similar to No. 136. Stunning tonal and rhythmic effects beginning at m. 76 created by the superimposition of a five-note against a four-note ascending and descending figure.

No. 143. Divided Arpeggios. Andante. (2' 5") T10 M11

Key center C; major and minor modes. Three-part variation form with introduction and coda. A study in arpeggiated four-note cross-relation chords (major and minor). Could serve as introductory material to No. 2 of the Bartók *Studies*, Op. 18, Sz. 72, and even has similarities to "pour les Arpèges composés" of the Debussy *Études*, Vol. II.

No. 144. Minor Seconds, Major Sevenths. Molto adagio, mesto. (3' 25") T9 M12

Key center E-flat. Free form, mostly mirror patterns between the hands. An atmospheric piece quite similar in sound to "Musiques Nocturnes" from *Out of Doors*, Sz. 81. Layered textures, a typical feature of Debussy's piano writing, consist basically of semitonal configurations and bell-like chords in sevenths. Much sensitivity and control of tone required for this delicate piece.

Nos. 145a and b. Chromatic Invention. Allegro. (1' 15" each) T9 M9

Key center D. Two voices in imitation (at the tritone!) and free counterpoint, in the style of the Bach inventions. Sections a and b are strict inversions of each other and thus can be played simultaneously (and quite effectively) on two pianos. Melodies are mainly based on the chromatic scale in five-finger position and thus present difficulties for the large hand. Measures are numbered for rehearsal purposes. Ensemble challenge with the long accelerando from m. 28 to the end of the piece; it must be gauged carefully to avoid a frantic conclusion.

No. 146. Ostinato. Vivacissimo. (2' 5") T12 M11

Key center D; mixed modes, mainly Dorian and Lydian. A multi-sectional virtuoso piece of the highest order. Can effectively end a recital or a Bartók group. The main unifying features are the Oriental-type melody,which is extensively varied, and the series of repeated chords and intervals in the left hand, which serve as a rhythmic backdrop. Bartók refers to "Bulgarian pipes" at m. 32.[24] Since this piece appears to include every conceivable touch indication and accent mark, it can serve as an effective textbook illustration of their usage.

No. 147. March. Allegro. (1' 45") T10 M7

Key center E. Octave triplets against heavy, ponderous ostinato figures in fourths and fifths. Difficult to make convincing. Some redistributions are suggested: at mm. 6–7, take the left-hand top voice with the right thumb; and at m. 10, break the chord with the left hand alone, leaving the right hand free to sustain the tones. Requires virtuoso octave and chord equipment.

Six Dances in Bulgarian Rhythm: Nos. 148–153

With the exception of Nos. 113 and 115 of the *Mikrokosmos*, these pieces are the only examples in Bartók's piano works based on Bulgarian folk music. Its most prominent feature is its non-symmetrical rhythmic patterns and mixed meters, resulting in fascinating and compelling rhythmic combinations. The set, dedicated to the British pianist Harriet Cohen, is most often played in public performance as a self-contained cycle.

No. 148. (1' 50") T12 M13

Key center E; combination of Aeolian and Phrygian modes. Extended melody over a sustained pedal on E, followed by variational treatment. Rhythmically flexible throughout, this is the only piece of the six that one can describe as lyrical, the remainder being cast in more of a perpetual-motion style. The meter signature of 4/8 + 2/8 + 3/8 should be strictly adhered to; the piece should not be played as 9/8. The MM markings fall out of the range of most metronomes; an alternative is to begin with 40 to the measure and change at m. 32 to quarter note = 120. Demands temperament, a good sense of rubato and tempo flexibility, and a well-developed octave technique.

No. 149. (1' 10") T10 M9

Key center C; pentatonic scale patterns. Light-textured, syncopated patterns in septuple meter with repeated-note figures. The indication "(Ped.)" at the beginning suggests that pedal be used at the player's discretion; and in this instance a shallow, semi-sustaining pedal is advised to maintain rhythmic clarity. Maintain a basically non-percussive touch throughout except where indicated otherwise ("martell." at m. 24, *sff* at m. 31). Give exact rhythmic definition at the very end (mm. 61–64), thinking the previous rhythmic pattern through the rests.

No. 150. (1' 20") T12 M11

Key center E, A; Lydian modes. Quintuple meter, scale figures alternating with sustained chordal sections. It is important that the eighth-note pulse be felt in the sustained sections (beginning in m. 5 and in similar sections). Particular attention should be given to the rhythmic tension created by the rhythmic grouping; too often one hears lethargic triplet rhythms. Measures 58–78 should be practiced slowly and carefully so that the extremely difficult rhythmic and contrapuntal combinations can be coordinated. A piece that calls for sharp contrasts in touch and temperament.

No. 151. (1' 25") T11 M10

Key center C; Lydian mode. Set of rhythmic variations on a pentatonic melody. One of the few instances when Bartók consciously alludes to his attraction for American folk music, specifically "the style of Gershwin."[25] Note the symmetrical rhythmic patterns of each measure in the melody. A light and playful atmosphere should be conveyed. The parallel triads beginning at m. 51 should be carefully fingered and the sudden dynamic changes beginning at m. 59 carefully observed.

No. 152. Allegro molto. (1' 13") T11 M10

Key center A; Lydian mode. Variational treatment of a staccato melody (note the key progression from A to B, C, and D before returning to A (at m. 25). A good study in staccato vs. legato. As in No. 148, pay close attention to the irregular rhythmic groupings to avoid a feeling of 9/8. Lightness and mobility required for this miniature scherzo.

No. 153. (1' 40") T12 M10

Key center E; mixed modes. Loose sonata design, much motivic development. The most virtuosic piece of the set. Requires good repetition, chord, and octave technique. The broken-octave figures in the left hand require light wrist movement, and a flexible thumb is needed in the repetition figures. Pay careful attention to the slur locations, giving a slight accentuation to the first note of each for rhythmic definition. This brilliant piece can serve not only as an effective finale to the six-part set, but can also end a recital program or a miscellaneous Bartók group.

Recordings

Hungaroton LPX 12326-B. *Bartók at the Piano*, Vol. I. Side 2, Band 5 (Nos. 124 and 146), 1937.

Hungaroton LPX 12330-A. *Bartók at the Piano*, Vol. I. Side 9, Band 1–6 (Nos. 113, 129, 131, 128, 120, 109, 138, 100, 142, 140, 133, 149, 148, 108, 150, 151, 94, 152, and 153), 1940.

Hungaroton LPX 12330-B. *Bartók at the Piano*, Vol. I. Side 10, Band 1–6 (Nos. 126, 116, 130, 139, 143, 147, 144, 97, 118, 141, 136, 125, and 114), 1940.

Hungaroton LPX 12333-B. *Bartók at the Piano*, Vol. I.

Turnabout/Vox THS 65010. *Bartók Plays Bartók*. Side 2, Band 1 (Nos. 2 [69 in original], 5 [127], and 6 [145] of *Seven Pieces From Mikrokosmos* for two pianos, four hands, Sz. 108), c. 1941.

Hungaroton LPX 12335-A. *Bartók Plays and Talks*, Vol. II. Side 3, Band 5
   (Nos. 138, 109, and 148), 1939.
Odyssey 32160220E (selections), 1968.

The following commentary is presented in the order that the pieces are listed
in the three Hungaroton collections. This sequence will facilitate the listening
procedure and may even provide ideas for innovative programming of some of
the *Mikrokosmos* selections.

No. 124: The tempo chosen is slow enough to accommodate the required
finger staccato for the "secco, quasi pizz." touch. A suspenseful effect is achieved
by delaying the crescendo until the penultimate measure.

No. 146: Pedal is used as indicated in the score, but never at the expense
of clarity; in mm. 28– 57 a melodic thread is always apparent, and interest is
always maintained by strict adherence to articulation markings and syncopations. At the "meno vivo" section (beginning in m. 81), there is virtually no
ritard until indicated at m. 104.

No. 113: The last eighth note of each measure is shortened somewhat to
give a sense of urgency to the downbeat of the next. The repetition is played
with the octave doublings suggested in the Notes and is introduced by a three-
measure bridge in which only the ostinato is played. In the coda the left hand
is played in octaves.

No. 129: The left-hand thirds at mm. 3, 6, 9, etc., lead into the next
downbeat with a slight crescendo to offset the right-hand syncopation. A light
scherzando approach is experienced throughout. At the "Tempo I" (beginning
in m. 54), the built-in ritard is made convincing by maintaining a metronomi-
cally exact tempo.

No. 131: Played a bit under tempo from the indication in the score (some-
where around quarter note = 116). Has a simple, folk-like quality. In mm.
35-42, pedal is used to give color to the accumulated sonorities, and from m.
46 to the end, the "ossia" version is chosen.

No. 128: The contrasts, both inherent in the writing and realized in the performance, give the piece the appearance of a set of character variations. The
opening is indeed played "pesante" with no attempt to refine phrasing. The
"Un poco più mosso" section is given a benign treatment but with slight, sudden accents where indicated. The "Meno mosso" section begins as a scherzo,
but builds in intensity to the end.

No. 120: The entire piece is devoid of percussiveness, with emphasis instead
on the lyrical aspects of the material. The parallel triads with staccato indications are detached only enough to go from chord to chord. The total effect is
lightness but not superficiality.

No. 109: The opening is given an almost legatissimo fluidity with much
rubato. The *f* dynamic at the "Risoluto" section is observed with the ensuing

ff in mind. The sostenuto pedal is used to sustain the sonorities at mm. 30 (released at m. 39) and 40.

No. 138: Whatever pedal is used is not noticeable until the "Più mosso" (beginning in m. 28), and even at that point it is used very sparingly. The accompaniment is presented throughout in clear detail, emphasizing whatever melodic importance it may have.

No. 100: One is always made aware of the expressive importance of each reappearance of the opening left-hand motive through dynamic emphasis, a slight delaying of the top note, or de-emphasis. A folk-like simplicity and rhythmic buoyancy are conveyed in the melody.

No. 142: The opening tempo is considerably faster than Bartók's MM marking (more like quarter note = 168). The "buzzing" effect is accomplished by emphasizing the melodic continuity of the larger note values (the accented dotted halves, which alternate between the hands), which are played a bit louder than the eighth-note figurations.

No. 140: In keeping with Bartók's performances of percussive pieces, accents are underplayed, the sound is intense without being raucous, and the dissonances are held in check by constant attention to the melodic direction of the moving voices.

No. 133: As in the previous example, there is no hint of stridency or harshness, mainly because of a fluid legato connecting the alternating chords and the modification of some of the loud dynamics (the *ff* at m. 18 and the *f* at m. 27 each seem two levels softer). Here again, the linear aspects are given priority.

No. 149: The total effect is one of lightness and fluidity. The pentatonic melody (beginning in m. 4) in the left hand is emphasized while the alternating statements in the right hand appear to be light embroidery. The only instance of pedal seems to be at its final indication (m. 55), and it is released only two measures before the end of the piece.

No. 148: Although this piece is the most lyrical of the "Six Dances in Bulgarian Rhythm," the element of dance and the steady metric pulse that it requires are always evident. Rubato effects are minimized except where indicated (beginning in mm. 28 and 44). The metric divisions of the opening section are de-emphasized in favor of fluidity of the ascending ostinato.

No. 108: As indicated in the opening indication, the *f* dynamic is consistent throughout, never losing intensity. The sforzandos are always brought out in relief from the other voices. One wonders why this piece was included in the midst of the Bulgarian dances in the recording sequence.

No. 150: The pedal is used to help the legato in the left-hand parallel sixths but does not adversely affect the clarity of the other counterpoint. Contrasts of lightness and intensity are convincingly communicated.

No. 151: The effect of the character variation form is presented by a vaudevillian series of mood and temperament contrasts. The softer sections give the effect of a scherzo, while the louder ones always maintain their clarity. No pedal is used at the alternating fortes (beginning in m. 60).

No. 94: This performance illustrates the legatissimo style of melodic delivery; there seems to be a slight, almost imperceptible, overlapping of the tones, effected either manually or by a controlled use of fragmentary pedals.

No. 152: Bartók is again successful in balancing the moving over the repeated voices in the alternating chord sections. The linear sections, by contrast (beginning in m. 16), are given an intense elasticity. In mm. 35–39 the octave doublings and the redistribution of registers seem to detract from the dynamic curve implicit in the section.

No. 153: The rhythmic ostinato in the left hand is underplayed in favor of a strong melodic delivery in the right. Two instances of a sudden dynamic drop (mm. 13 and 58) intensify the crescendos that follow. In the final three measures, the triple-octave melody in the upper voices is not abruptly cut off, as would seem to be indicated, but blends in with the E-major sustained chord.

No. 126: Up to m. 21 the chord progressions are played as legato as possible without connecting pedal, creating a certain weightiness in keeping with the "pesante" indication. Beginning at m. 21, the execution is leggiero and detached until the crescendo eight measures later.

No. 116: The variations undergo very subtle character transformations, each one becoming more expressive and rhythmically more flexible than the previous one. The introductory statement is very straightforward at first but becomes reflective as a bridge statement and quite climactic as a postlude.

No. 130: The humor in this piece is conveyed mainly by slight dynamic changes with each melodic fragment that go beyond the printed indications.

No. 139: An effective counterpart to No. 130. Here again, the animated portrayal is enhanced by a continuously changing dynamic scheme within a limited range.

No. 143: Despite the use of pedal, the arpeggios maintain a melodic clarity and definition, never yielding to a filigree-type execution. Pedal is used throughout the piece; it is not limited to the few instances on the first page where it is indicated.

No. 147: Because of constant tonal balance in favor of the moving voices, the sound impression is more of two-voice counterpoint and linear movement than of the ponderous monotony of a march.

No. 144: Although the piece recalls the style of Debussy, the delicately veiled sonorities that one would expect are abandoned in favor of a clearly and boldly articulated sound. The total effect is one of intensity rather than subtlety.

No. 97: Here again, the use of pedal does not obscure the melody. The swaying arpeggio figures assume the role of counterpoint rather than mere accompaniment and sometimes even overshadow the "cantabile" melodic statements.

No. 118: The seeming monotony of two-voice counterpoint and a continuous rhythmic figure is relieved in this performance by a wide variety of colors and expressive effects. Except for the one *sf* (m. 6), all the accent marks are reinforced by a crescendo or are underplayed, resulting in a continuous melodic flow.

No. 141: Dynamics, moods, tempos, and registers are continuously varied within one basic four-voice texture. The sustained tonic tones are heavily accented at first but eventually yield to accents and slurs in the outer voices. The principle of variety within unity is admirably displayed here.

No. 136: The technique of parallel and mirror counterpoint vs. sustained tones, as found in No. 141, is again presented in this example, making the pair effective as companion pieces. The performance guidelines in No. 141 are reinforced here.

No. 125: An attempt is made to keep the repeated melodic patterns even in sonority and to give more expressiveness to those of melodic interest. This is especially noticeable when the accompaniment figures, repetitious at first, evolve into melodies of their own (beginning in mm. 15 and 28).

No. 114: The two- and four-note slur groupings in mm. 1, 9, and 17 are played with a slight lift between them. The folklike theme and its inversion are given a rather weighty and straightforward treatment, with accented tenutos.

Notes

1. BBES, pp. 427–28.
2. Ibid., p. 432.
3. Ibid., p. 428.
4. CROW, p. 139.
5. *Tempo*, 1967/68, 12.
6. SUGU, p. 22.
7. Ibid., p. 25.
8. Ibid., p. 34.
9. Ibid., p. 41.
10. Ibid., p. 43.
11. BBES, p. 382.
12. SUGU, p. 58.
13. Ibid., p. 73.
14. Ibid., p. 79.
15. Ibid., p. 88.
16. Ibid., p. 97.
17. Ibid., p. 98.
18. Ibid., p. 99.
19. Ibid., p. 100.
20. Ibid., p. 111.
21. Ibid., p. 115.
22. Ibid., p. 120.
23. Ibid., p. 125.
24. Ibid., p. 130.
25. Ibid., p. 138.

APPENDIX A
Solo Piano Works in Order
of Difficulty

Technical (T-rating)

Sz.	Range	Average	Classification
53	1–4	2.5	Elementary
107, I	1–4	2.5	
107, II	2–5	3.5	
35a	4–6	5	
42, I	2–8	5	
42, II	3–7	5	
57, I	3–8	5.5	
107, III	3–8	5.5	Intermediate
57, II	4–9	6.5	
66	5–8	6.5	
39	2–12	7	
38	4–11	7.5	
45	6–9	7.5	
55	5–10	7.5	
56	5–10	7.5	
71	3–12	7.5	
107, IV	5–10	7.5	
44	4–12	8	
107, V	6–10	8	
82	5–12	8.5	
105	7–12	9.5	
62	7–13	10	
74	6–14	10	
84	9–11	10	
107, VI	8–12	10	
47	9–12	10.5	
21	11	11	Advanced
77	7–15	11	
22	10–14	12	
49	12	12	
43	12–13	12.5	
80	10–15+	12.5	
81	10–15+	12.5	
41	13–14	13.5	
46	13–14	13.5	
72	14–15+	14.5	
26	15	15	

Musical (M-rating)

Sz.	Range	Average	Classification
107, I	1–3	2	Elementary
53	1–5	3	
107, II	2–5	3.5	
42, I	2–6	4	
57, I	3–6	4.5	
57, II	3–6	4.5	
107, III	3–7	5	
42, II	3–8	5.5	
56	4–7	5.5	
107, IV	4–8	6	Intermediate
55	4–9	6.5	
107, V	4–9	6.5	
35a	5–9	7	
39	3–11	7	
38	4–11	7.5	
44	4–11	7.5	
71	4–11	7.5	
49	8	8	
66	7–9	8	
82	5–11	8	
105	6–11	8.5	
21	10	10	
45	10	10	
47	9–12	10.5	
62	9–12	10.5	
84	10–11	10.5	
22	10–12	11	Advanced
43	11	11	
107, VI	9–13	11	
72	9–14	11.5	
77	9–14	11.5	
81	8–15	11.5	
46	11–14	12.5	
74	11–14	12.5	
26	13	13	
41	14	14	
80	13–15	14	

APPENDIX B
Publishers' Addresses

Alfred Publishing Co., Inc., 15335 Morrison Street, Sherman Oaks, CA 91403.

Associated Music Publishers, Inc., 866 Third Avenue, New York, NY 10022.

Belwin-Mills Publishing Corp., 25 Deshon Drive, Melville, NY 11746. (K-BM)

Boosey & Hawkes, Inc., 200 Smith Street, Farmingdale, NY 11735. (B&H)

Bradley Publications, distributed by Raydiola Music.

California Music Press, distributed by Hansen Music House.

CH II Music and Books, Ltd., distributed by Hansen Music House.

Clef Music Publishing Corp., 315 West 57 Street, New York, NY 10019.

Dover Publications, 180 Varick Street, New York, NY 10014.

Editio Musica Budapest, distributed by B&H. (EMB)

Carl Fischer, Inc., 62 Cooper Square, New York, NY 10003.

General Words & Music Co., distributed by Neil A. Kjos Music Co.

Hansen Music House, P.O. Box 42069, San Francisco, CA 94142.

International Music Corp., 511 Fifth Avenue, New York, NY 10017.

Edwin F. Kalmus, distributed by K-BM.

Neil A. Kjos Music Co., 4382 Jutland Drive, San Diego, CA 92117.

Edward B. Marks Music Corp., 1619 Broadway, 11th floor, New York, NY 10019.

Music Sales Corp., 24 East 22 Street, New York, NY 10010.

Theodore Presser Co., Presser Place, Bryn Mawr, PA 19010.

Pro Art Publishing, Inc., distributed by K-BM.

Raydiola Music (c/o Warner Bros.), 9000 Sunset Boulevard, Los Angeles, CA 90069.

Julius Rózsavölgyi, distributed by B&H. (EMB, Budapest)

Károly Rózsnyai, distributed by B&H. (EMB, Budapest)

G. Schirmer, Inc., 866 Third Avenue, New York, NY 10022.

B. Schott's Söhne, Weihergarten 5, 6500 Mainz, West Germany.

Schroeder & Gunther, distributed by Associated Music Publishers.

Studio P/R, 224 South Lebanon Street, Lebanon, IN 46052.

Universal Edition (London, Vienna, Zurich), distributed by B&H. (UE)

Willis Music Co., 7380 Industrial Road, Florence, KY 41042.

Yorktown Music Press (London), distributed by Music Sales Corp.

APPENDIX C
Editions and Transcriptions
by Bartók of Keyboard Works
by Other Composers

Bach, Johann Sebastian. *The Well-Tempered Clavier*, Vols. I and II. EMB. For pedagogical purposes, this edition presents the 48 preludes and fugues in order of difficulty rather than in the key-related sequence in the original.

Bach, Johann Sebastian. *Sonata VI*, BWV. 530. Rózsavölgyi.

Beethoven, Ludwig van. *Sonata in C-sharp minor*, Op. 27, No. 2. EMB.

Beethoven, Ludwig van. *Bagatelles*, Op. 33; *Variations*, Op. 34; *Polonaise*, Op. 89; *Bagatelles*, Op. 119. Rózsnyai.

Chopin, Frédéric. *Waltzes*. Rózsnyai.

Ciaia, Azzolino Bernardino della. *Sonata in G major*. Carl Fischer.

Couperin, François. *Selected Keyboard Works*. EMB.

Couperin, François. *Eighteen Pieces*. Rózsnyai.

Duvernoy, V. A. *Etude du Mécanisme*. Bard.

Frescobaldi, Girolamo. *Toccata in G major. Fuga in G minor*. Carl Fischer.

Handel, George Frederic. *Sonatas*. Rózsnyai.

Haydn, Franz Joseph. *Sonata No. 53 in E minor*, Hob. XVI/34. EMB.

Heller, Stephen. *Etudes*, Opp. 45, 46, 47, and 125; *Tarantella*; *Album*, Vols. I, II, and III. Rózsavölgyi.

Marcello, Benedetto. *Sonata in B-flat major*. Carl Fischer.

Mendelssohn, Felix. *Scherzo in B minor*; *Prelude and Fugue in E major*. Rózsnyai.

Mozart, Wolfgang Amadeus. *Sonatas for Piano*, Vols. I and II (complete). EMB.

Mozart, Wolfgang Amadeus. *Twenty Sonatas*. K-BM.

Mozart, Wolfgang Amadeus. *Sonata in A major*, K. 331. ("Marcia alla Turka" published separately.) EMB.

Mozart, Wolfgang Amadeus. *Sonata in G major*, K. 545. EMB.

Rossi, Michelangelo. *Toccata No. 1 in C major*; *Toccata No. 2 in A minor*. Carl Fischer.

Scarlatti, Domenico. *Selected Sonatas*, Vols. I and II. EMB.

Scarlatti, Domenico. *Five Pieces*. K-BM.

Scarlatti, Domenico. *Essercizi*. Rózsnyai.

Schubert, Franz. *Sonata in G major*; *Sonata in A minor*; *Two Scherzi*. Rózsnyai.

Schumann, Robert. *Album for the Young*. Rózsnyai.

Zipoli, Domenico. *Pastorale in C major*. Carl Fischer.

APPENDIX D
Critical Survey of Teaching Editions and Collections of Bartók's Piano Music

Agay, Denes, ed. *Bartók Is Easy! 15 Melodious Pieces for the Young Pianist*. Presser. Compiled from Sz. 39 and 42. Simplistic title may mislead a younger student. The editor has added, deleted, or changed some original indications, often in disagreement even with the differences between the first and second editions of Sz. 42. Some invented titles do not capture the essential spirit of the piece. Most difficult piece is "Bear Dance," Sz. 39, No. 10.

Agay, Denes, ed. *The Joy of Bartók*. Yorktown. Compiled from Sz. 38, 39, 42 (Vols. I and II), 44, 45, 52, and 53. An attractive and varied assortment of 51 pieces graded in approximate order of difficulty. Titles both original and invented. Except for occasional omissions of pedaling and accent indications, the pieces are faithful to the original texts.

Alfred, publ., *Bartók. 24 of his Easiest Piano Pieces*. Compiled from Sz. 39, 42 (Vols. I and II), and 53. Aside from a few added interpretive indications and titles and some MM markings that are different from Bartók's, this collection is quite accurate. Almost every piece is preceded by brief explanations and interpretive suggestions. Selections appear in order of difficulty, the last piece being "Evening in the Country," Sz. 39, No. 5.

Alfred, publ., *Bartók. 24 of his Most Popular Piano Pieces*. Compiled from Sz. 38, 39, 42 (Vols. I and II), 44, 53, and 55. Also listed is *Rhapsody*, with a date of 1904, but this is really Nos. 40 and 41 of Vol. II of Sz. 42, not Sz. 26. This collection is probably meant as a more difficult sequel to *24 of his Easiest Piano Pieces*, although there are some duplications. It is unfortunate that not all the pieces are identified as to which collection they originally came from.

Anson, George, ed. *Anson Introduces Bartók* (Vol. I, Elementary; Vol. II, Intermediate). Willis. Compiled from Sz. 39, 42 (Vols. I and II), and 53. Some unnecessary fingerings and pedal markings have been added, although the original indications remain unaltered. "Hand Position" fingering charts accompany some of the easier pieces, as in the early volumes of *Mikrokosmos*. MM markings are omitted, even though they appear in the original editions. The remarks that precede each piece give practice and interpretive suggestions that are often helpful but are more often banal and patronizing. Large notation actually makes for more difficult reading.

Balógh, Ernö, ed. *Béla Bartók. Selected Works for the Piano*. G. Schirmer. Contains Sz. 21, 26, 38, 41, 44, 43, 45, 47, and 55. Similar to an urtext edition but should be compared with parallel examples in the Suchoff (BBPI) and K-BM editions because of slight differences in tempo indications and MM markings. Only the more advanced pianist should consider buying this collection.

Banowetz, Joseph, ed. *Béla Bartók. An Introduction to the Composer and his Music*. Kjos.

Contains Sz. 42, Vol. I. Although this is an edition of a single work, it deserves special commendation for its informative introduction on Bártok's life and the history of Hungarian music, its concise English translations of folk texts, and its impeccable editing of the music.

Bradley, publ., *Béla Bartók. Piano Pieces in Their Original Form.* Eight pieces compiled from Sz. 39, 42, and 53. Large notation, invented titles. Adheres closely to original indications.

Brimhall, John, ed. *My Favorite Bartók.* CH II. Twenty-one pieces compiled from Sz. 53, 42, and 39. Attractive and reliable collection and an affordable purchase. Identifies collection to which each piece belongs.

Chapman, Ernest, ed. *Béla Bartók. A Highlight Collection of His Original Piano Works.* California Music Press, Inc. (Maestro). Compiled from Sz. 22, 38, 39, 41, 42, and 43. Twelve-page introduction includes a biographical sketch, photographs, maps, illustrations, and explanatory notes on the works presented. Presents a good cross-section of Bartók's earlier works of varying levels of difficulty. Follows closely the format of the Kail edition, both of them being urtext reprints of the early editions and equally affordable. One might prefer this collection because of the generous biographical information it offers.

EMB, publ., *Bartók Béla. Album.* Vol. I: Sz. 38 (Nos. 2, 3, 5, 10, and 14), 47 (Nos. 1 and 2), 43 (No. 1), 44 (Nos. 1, 2, 5, and 6), and 39 (Nos. 5 and 10). Vol. II: Sz. 46, 39 (Nos. 3, 7, and 8), 38 (Nos. 1, 6, 8, and 11), 43 (No. 1), 47 (No. 3), 44 (No. 7), 35a, and 45 (No.3). Vol. III: Sz. 38 (Nos. 4, 7, 9, 12, and 13), 39 ("Dedication" and Nos. 2 and 6), 44 (Nos. 3 and 4), 45 (Nos. 1, 2, and 4), 55, and 41. This collection was selected by Bartók before his emigration to the United States in 1940 and was first published by Rózsavölgyi & Co. in 1947. The edition is of course impeccably edited, and the order of individual selections (parts of a single work may be distributed over all three volumes; see especially Sz. 38 and 39) provides a uniformity of mood and suggests programming possibilities.

EMB, publ., *Béla Bartók. Young People at the Piano* (Vols. I and II). Compiled from Sz. 39 and 42 (Vols. I and II). Vol. II contains ten pieces "for the second and third years of instruction." Reliable collection with pieces arranged in an attractive performing sequence.

Frank, Marcel, ed. *Bartók. The Best in Music Made Easy for Piano.* Clef. Compiled from Sz. 42 and 39. A difficult edition to read because of the narrow spacing between the staves and the awkward fingering locations. Disregards Bartók's original markings in favor of editorial indications that are random, ambiguous, and often contradictory to his musical intentions.

Goldberger, David, ed. *The Easy Piano Music of Béla Bartók.* Schroeder & Gunther. Compiled from Sz. 38, 39, 42 (Vols. I and II), 44, and 53. Short biographical sketch. Careful selection of pieces and good editing, the latter consisting of added fingerings, MM markings in the absence of Bartók's, pedal markings, and clarifying notation. Some of the fingerings are viable alternatives to Bartók's own, the added MM markings are in brackets rather than in parentheses, and all other emendations are done with taste and a regard for musical intent. The original collections from which the pieces were taken are not identified, but the individual works are arranged with effective programming in mind.

Kail, Robert, ed. *Béla Bartók. His Greatest Piano Solos.* Copa. Includes Sz. 42, 39,

38, 22 (Nos. 2, 3, and 4), and 44 (No. 5). Adhering closely to "the original Hungarian editions," this collection offers a good cross-section of Bartók's piano music written between 1903 and 1910. It follows the format of the Chapman edition, which was also a reprint of the early editions.

K-BM, publ., *Bartók. An Album for Piano Solo.* Includes Sz. 35a, 22 (Nos. 2 and 4), 43, 55, 38, 44, and 39 (No. 10). Similar to an urtext edition but should be compared with the Suchoff (BBPI) and Balógh (Schirmer) editions because of slight differences in tempo and MM markings. Offers a good cross-section of Bartók's earlier and more difficult piano works.

Nevin, Mark, ed. *Bartók for the Young Pianist.* Pro Art. Compiled from Sz. 39, 38, 42, and 53. Twenty-one selections of approximately increasing difficulty, ending with "Bear Dance," Sz. 39, No. 10. This collection should be compared with a more reliable, original edition, since there are many additions, changes, and even deletions from Bartók's own indications, none of them acknowledged by the editor.

Novik, Ylda, ed. *Young Pianist's Guide to Bartók.* Studio P/R. Compiled from Sz. 42 and 53. The one-page biographical sketch de-emphasizes the tragedies in Bartók's life and concentrates on his accomplishments. The titles of the sixteen selections are invented, and no indication is given as to which collection they are taken from. Photos and commentary adorn most pieces. Some of the explanatory notes as to dance types and folk tune texts are helpful, but others are simplistic. Contains performance suggestions such as balance and redistributions. Freely edited but to no adverse effect. Enclosed recording by the editor of the selections in the volume is a welcome feature; the total effect of the performance is non-percussive, almost fragile.

Palmer, Willard A., ed. *Bartók. An Introduction to his Piano Works.* Alfred. Compiled from Sz. 39, 42, 44, and 53. Thirty-one pieces presented in order of difficulty, with "Bear Dance," Sz. 39, No. 10, ending the collection. Includes some of Bartók's written commentary and illustrations from Sz. 52, in which wrist and finger action, touch schemes, accents, and syncopations are explained. Each piece is preceded by a capsule summary of the folk text. Performance suggestions relative to Bartók's remarks in Sz. 52 preface each piece. Editorial indications (fingerings, redistributions for small hands) are indicated in grey print. A highly recommended collection.

Palmer, Willard A., ed. *Bartók. The First Book for Young Pianists.* Alfred. Compiled from Sz. 42 and 52. A more concise and elementary version of Palmer's *Introduction*, but containing the same careful and tasteful editing and interpretive suggestions. Short introductory section explains wrist action and finger staccato. Some of the folk arrangements contain a "sing-along" text above the notation. One of the best elementary Bartók collections in print.

Palmer, Willard A., ed. *Béla Bartók. Selected Children's Pieces for the Piano.* Alfred. Compiled from Sz. 39, 42, and 53. Thirteen pieces "carefully selected [and] arranged in approximate order of difficulty." Some of Bartók's original fingerings and "indefinite [?]" dynamic indications have been modified for clarity. Measure numbers and widely spaced printing are helpful for the student. Not as reliable an edition as Palmer's *Introduction.*

Philipp, Isidor, ed. *Bartók. 16 Pieces for Children.* International. Includes pieces not only from Sz. 42, as its name implies, but from Sz. 38 (including No. 4, which is hardly a children's piece) and 39. Fingerings altered from Bartók's original, but worthy of consideration.

Richter, Ada, ed. *Bartók, Early Works.* Warner Bros. Compiled from Sz. 39, 42 (Vols. I and II), and 53.

BBPI: Suchoff, Benjamin, ed. *Piano Music of Béla Bartók* (Series I and II). Dover. Includes all the solo piano works from Sz. 21 through 55. The most monumental scholarly edition of Bartók's early piano works ever assembled in the United States. A Bartók centennial project (published 1981), this collection represents "the only edition of the great Hungarian composer to be based on corrections from his memorabilia or original editions in the New York Bartók Archive." This two-volume collection contains extensive background information for each work, reproductions from Bartók's own scholarly publications of original folk tunes, folk text translations, and manuscript reproductions for certain works. No serious Bartók pianist or scholar can do without this highly valuable, but affordable, collection edited by one of the foremost Bartók scholars in America.

SELECTED BIBLIOGRAPHY

Antokoletz, Elliott. *The Music of Béla Bartók*. Berkeley: University of California Press, 1985.

BANO: Banowetz, Joseph. *The Pianist's Guide to Pedaling*. Bloomington: Indiana University Press, 1985.

Bartók, Béla. *Centenary Edition of Bartók's Records*. Vol. I: *Bartók at the Piano, 1920–1945*. Hungaroton LPX 12326-33, 1981.

Bartók, Béla. *Centenary Edition of Bartók's Records*. Vol. II: *Bartók Plays and Talks, 1912–1944*. Hungaroton LPX 12334-38, 1981.

Bartók, Béla. *Bartók Béla. Complete Edition*. Vol. II: Piano Music, Nos. 1–8. Hungaroton LPX 1299, 1300, 11335-38, 11394-95, 11405-407. Jacket notes by János Demény (No. 1); László Somfai (Nos. 2, 3, and 6); István Szelényi (Nos. 4 and 5). All translations by Rosemarie Prockl.

BBES: Bartók, Béla. *Essays*. Edited by Benjamin Suchoff. New York: St. Martin's Press, 1976.

BBHU: Bartók, Béla. *The Hungarian Folk Song*. Edited by Benjamin Suchoff. Albany: State University of New York Press, 1981.

BBLE: Bartók, Béla. *Letters*. Edited by János Demény. London: Faber & Faber; New York: St. Martin's Press, 1971.

BBPI: Bartók, Béla. *Piano Music of Béla Bartók*. The Archive Edition, edited by Benjamin Suchoff. Series I and II. New York: Dover Publications, Inc., 1981.

Bartók, Béla. *Piano Music*, Vols. I, II, and III. Performed by György Sándor. Vox SVBX 5425-47, 1961.

BBRO: Bartók, Béla. *Rumanian Folk Music*. Vol. I: Instrumental Melodies; Vol. IV: Carols and Christmas Songs. Edited by Benjamin Suchoff. The Hague: Martinus Nijhoff, 1967.

BBSL: Bartók, Béla. *Slovenské Ludové Piesne* (Slovakian Folk Songs), Vols. I and II. Bratislava: Academia Scientiarum Slovaca, 1959.

Bator, Victor. *The Béla Bartók Archives. History and Catalogue*. New York: Bartók Archives Publication, 1963.

CROW: Crow, Todd, ed. *Bartók Studies*. Detroit: Detroit Reprints in Music, 1976.

FENY: Fenyo, Thomas. "The Piano Music of Béla Bartók." Ph.D. diss., University of California, Los Angeles, 1956.

Fuchss, Werner. *Béla Bartók und die Schweiz*. Bern: Nationale Schweizerische UNESCO-Kommission, 1973.

Gerig, Reginald R. *Famous Pianists and Their Technique*. Washington, D.C.: Robert B. Luce, 1974.

GRIF: Griffiths, Paul. *Bartók*. London: J. M. Dent, 1984.

Haraszti, Emil. *Béla Bartók, His Life and Works*. Paris: Lyrebird Press, 1938.

Hinson, Maurice. *Guide to the Pianist's Repertoire*. Bloomington: Indiana University Press, 1973; 2d, rev. and enl. ed., 1987.

Hodges, Janice Kay Gray. "The Teaching Aspects of Bartók's Mikrokosmos." A.Mus.D. diss., University of Texas at Austin, 1974.

Horn, Herbert Alvin. "Idiomatic Writing of the Piano Music of Béla Bartók." A.Mus.D. diss. University of Southern California, 1963.

Hundt, Theodor. *Bartóks Satztechnik in den Klavierwerken.* Regensburg: Gustav Bosse Verlag, 1971.

KROO: Kroó, György. *A Guide to Bartók.* Budapest: Corvina Press, 1974; Vienna: Universal Edition, 1974.

Lindlar, Heinrich. *Lübbes Bartók Lexikon.* Bergisch Gladbach, West Germany: Gustav Lübbe Verlag, 1984.

Milne, Hamish. *Bartók, His Life and Times.* New York: Hippocrene Books, 1982.

Moreux, Serge. *Béla Bartók.* London: Harvill Press, 1953.

The New Grove Dictionary of Music and Musicians. Edited by Stanley Sadie. London: Macmillan, 1980.

Scott, Emily Jane. "The Rumanian Folk Melody in Bartók's *Rumanian Folk Dances and Sonatina*." M.M. thesis, University of Texas at Austin, 1973.

SIKI: Siki, Béla. *Piano Repertoire. A Guide to Interpretation and Performance.* New York: Schirmer Books, 1981.

SODO: Somfai, László, ed. *Documenta Bartókiana*, Vol. VI. Budapest: Akadémiai Kiadó, 1981.

SORO: Somfai, László, ed. *Two Rumanian Dances [Sz. 43] for Piano.* (Reprint of the original manuscript.) Budapest: Editio Musica Budapest, 1974.

STEV: Stevens, Halsey. *The Life and Music of Béla Bartók.* London, Oxford, and New York: Oxford University Press, 1953, 1964.

SUGU: Suchoff, Benjamin. *Guide to the Mikrokosmos.* New York: Boosey and Hawkes, 1971.

Szabolcsi, Bence. *Béla Bartók, sa vie et son oeuvre.* Budapest: Corvina; Leipzig: Breitkopf & Härtel, 1957.

UJFA: Ujfalussy, József. *Béla Bartók.* Boston: Crescendo Publishing Co., 1971.

Wolters, Klaus. *Handbuch der Klavierliteratur zu zwei Händen.* Zurich: Atlantis Verlag, 1977.

INDEX